WHY BIRDS SING AT DAWN

Why Birds Sing at Dawn

Embracing Death and Change as Transformation

JULIE J. HIGHTMAN

Julie J. Hightman

COPYRIGHT

The events and conversations in this book have been set down to the best of the author's ability and permissions have been granted by those named who were reachable for contact.

First Paperback Edition April 2022
Cover Art & Design by Julie Hightman
Technical Cover Design by Brendon Carl
ISBN: 979-8-9860242-0-2 (Paperback)
ISBN: 979-8-9860242-1-9 (ebook)
Library of Congress Control Number: 2022908494

Published by Julie Hightman
www.faizhealing.net/books
Portland, OR, USA

"To all my loves lost in form but not in spirit"

"My Sweet Flower
I journey in time
To see your petals fall
To feel your wind whispering
Like sunlight rising over death
With the moon I will sing
In repose of this Dream-
After night, comes Morning
And I know
Love gifts Eternity.

-Julie J.

TRIBUTES

These pages are a tribute to the 34 Dear Ones in my life that have crossed the threshold between life and death from 2012-2021. May their memory be spoken of often with gratitude.

2012- *Ralph Kirk*
2013- *Randy Hansen*
2014- *Azrael, Hunter, Christine Hightman*
2015- *Angela Decorte, Terri Grant-Post, Ted Hightman*
2016- *Amaunet, Tansy, Kathy Brineman, Divinity*
2017- *Steve Gunther, Scott Brineman, Bob Chin, Halo, Kyoto*
2018- *Nutmeg, Cloud, Snow, Sandra Bloom, Lucia*
2019- *Alison Henderson, Igneous, Kathy Shore, Peter Winterfield, Victor Drower, Judy Drower*
2020- *Hugh Morris, Ralph Baird*
2021- *Kriya, Talon, Mike Biagini, Quetesh*

CONTENTS

Introduction:

Death Opens the Gate to Transformation

Every death is unique in its' own way. The experience of death may change our perceptions of death itself, someone we knew, and life as we live it. If we are capable of objectivity in our emotional perceptions about intensity, purpose, and lingering desires, we can allow ourselves to honor the experience in connection to those we have lost in a healing way. Lingering in the details of each circumstance around a death is a natural part of the grieving process. No one else can tell you how to grieve or the length of time you should take to grieve. Whether we face the death as it happens or we avoid facing reality for a time, the emotional loss exists inside us either way. It can consume us in conscious or unconscious ways.

For many, death has a way of skewing our awareness of time. Time may seem like it is increasing or decreasing in the pace of life and mind exponentially. Some have very clear memory of the experience at the time of loss or sobering reflections that come or go during the process. Regarding these beautiful moments as treasures for understanding and empowering keys revealed by the mind and soul is an essential part of healing.

There may be times when our hearts linger in the storm of emotion; heavy and waiting for the tumult to end. The empty space in the heart allowing "light-heartedness", where receptivity and openness is free flowing, becomes full of many voices and feelings. It becomes less empty in a positive, open, and light enabled way. This is the paradigm of a light heart and a heavy heart revealed through many actions by our own choosing. This choice may be methodical or spontaneous through the conscious or subconscious motivations we employ.

We may not see it immediately if we are avoiding but others may see and sense it directly. The strength of personality will dictate the storm we carry; holding it contained or outwardly brewing around everything in our lives. It may be nuanced by self-sabotaging opportunities for empowerment, outbursts of emotion that flutter with irrationality, solidified walls of self-focus and avoidance of intimacy, or combinations of these and other responses that are a short term fix yet an unhealthy answer for the long term. At best, the response to death and loss can be graceful, surrendering with relief and inspiration for renewal. It can come with the clarity of calm acceptance bringing solace in the way we view life as a creative force. Renewal and rebirth require deconstruction and degradation of a creature or concept in order to continue the cycle of creation in one form or another. It is evident in the cycles we see on this planet that all life gives back to all life. The creation of new life requires significant resources to perform. No matter how hard it is as conscious beings to witness the withering and the sudden deaths of our loved ones and parts of our world, the truth of the cycle chants perpetually.

We can choose to be an active part of this cycle and empower our lives with continued renewals for inspired creativity or we can choose to wither like those we have lost. This process may be slow or fast, depending on how caught up we are in our emotional turmoil or anhedonia. Why then do we exist if we cannot continue to take an active part in life? Is it because we fear living? Is it because we are mired by illusion, repeating the intensity of our sorrow in loss, as though we were the one lost or dead? Have we lost ourselves? Perhaps, we have found an emptiness we cannot fill in our mind's eye to move forward. The emotions are too strong, weighing us down. At times, it feels this way. At times it is just going through the motions, uncertain of how to feel; the emotions locked inside. Other times it is a wash of emotions misplaced and overly sensitized. How do we move from a heavy-hearted experience back into a lighthearted state to continue a passionate life?

....

The recognition of every death ushers in a kaleidoscope of feelings. There are similarities and parallels, but every death touches us in specific ways. The feelings are a cascade of emotion that can unravel in different orders and intensities depending on our attachments. The cords of love and affection, of a sense of necessity to share and experience life with who we have lost, may be many or few, weak or strong. The links that remind us of previous experiences with love or fear may induce a greater sense of suffering. The current circumstances in our lives surrounding and contributing to our mental emotional load, often deeply affects how much one feels overdrawn with attention to stress and creates resistance to the acts of tending oneself, in order to heal more gracefully. Yet, the hallmarks of circumstance may be enough to unsettle our deepest awareness of peace and acceptance as we get trapped in the mind, cycling disturbing parts of our story. Every death is special. It is worth acknowledging and honoring this in the process of sorting thoughts and emotions that come through about the death one is experiencing.

Some deaths are tragic and shocking. Someone or something may be taken quickly out of this plane of existence without warning. Whether quick and peaceful in comparison to fast and turbulent, the shock is the same. Some essence we held moments ago has now departed and the whole of our being can feel it. It is not uncommon for people who are very connected in their heart cords to feel or to know the moment their loved one has left this plane. Some dream it. Others feel the urge to reach out to them or just know something feels wrong inside about this connection. It is later when we really begin to analyze and rationalize what happened that we pick it apart, judge it, and choose to hold onto it or let it go. It can be a cycle of conviction or confusion. When this manifests it is a block to refining the fluid substance of free emotion.

Witnessing a loved one's expected passing into death can also feel tragic. The shock of watching them endure pain and struggle to live in their body as it breaks down over a period of weeks or months involves more focus on them directly, whether you are a bystander or caregiver. When they pass the process of sorting arises, even if this has already been happening throughout the duration of their last days. The moment their spirit releases itself from body is the same moment that we acknowledge a part of the connection to this essence within us is relinquished.

These tragic deaths weigh on the psyche with some layer of obscurity we cannot reach, a murky cloud dispensing itself into the waters of the mind and dousing the fire of the heart. It is as though some injustice is unresolved. Returning to the routines of normalcy with a positive outlook meets resistance and an awkward mixture of languid disinterest blended with a compulsive need to stay focused on something other than our pain and confusion. With shock, the stunned lack of sensation and complete acknowledgment that something is different may also be present. It is a state to feel through once the malaise has passed and we find strength in accepting what is no longer.

Yet, some deaths are a graceful return into the veils. As elders grow old and begin to decline, physically and mentally, we watch their beauty in staying present with life beyond their aches and pains until they are no longer capable of saluting the day with a bright eye and jovial mouth. They may linger in their physical body, but their heart and mind begin to rest more deeply in longer cycles until it is automatic, even when they are speaking in conversation or eating. Their flame grows dimmer. They come to acknowledge they are no longer living, just existing. When it comes time for them to release a final breath their heart slows like a pilgrim easing into the final stages of a journey. It quickens with anticipation at select moments, becoming more irregular as the breath follows in rhythm. The spirit moves out in tidal flow and then it is gone. The light from the body is extinguished. A sense of ease and grace has filled them as well as the cord between you and them. All feels right in this ending. Even the tides of emotion break through and out of your being. It is an expected waveform that is clearer in its resonance, deep within the song of emotion beating in your heart. The mind can see the mercy in this death and the grace and wisdom of its hand in life. With honor and acknowledgement, the stories of the elders may be cherished forever. The wisdom of their generation becomes encapsulated and fortified by what we have taken in as our own truth and perpetuated.

~The Interdependence of Morale, Mortality, and Immortality~

Many would argue that faith and belief are the cause of one's resilience or disempowerment to the point of despair. When spirituality and science vie for the lead in one's mind, creating clarity or obscurity in truth and fallacy, one's rationalizations are often compartmentalized without full integration. The rules we perceive in life are founded in our orientation to the contexts of living and the expressions of others we witness in their orientation to it. If someone is no longer able to be a witness of others, they lose the objective input that is inherent in the awareness of other stories, practices, and responses that teach or influence us into another state of creativity. Creativity is what revitalizes our morale and our perspectives on mortality.

If we lose the witness of self we lose the objective awareness of our own subjectivity and become immersed only in the experience of that subjectivity. Any further actions we make for the good of self, in the face of self, or in the face of circumstance is obscured. The maintenance of both forms of objective allows the creative mind to still ask questions to expand in greater acceptance and awareness of how self is in the world. This is directly applicable to experiences that challenge morality and mortality. When one feels a loss or a diminishing of passion, the perception of will is intertwined with resilience or defeat. Actively seeking out love and connection for reflection and playtime to reinvigorate release is an essential asset in the enlightenment of our passion within. Resilience and defeat may still operate as feelings within self but be transformed into "something" more expansive and less confining subjectively. This "operable something" may arise in specific contexts or from a consistent belief we apply, but both are influenced and substantiated by creativity. Creativity is a skillful power led by the re-enlightened passion that loving connection and play have to offer.

Every day is a new day to choose how we want to orient ourselves to the experience of existence. One can choose an open heart with gratitude and graceful strength or any other emotional box of resistance. The choice to expand or contract is there in every moment. How we carry our accountability around our receptivity and willingness to resolve the dissonance or to be the dissonance during times of hardship affects our integrity of self and our integrity with others. It also affects the outcome of circumstances and may be the key that opens or shuts doors in the material world we seek to manifest our dreams in and the psyche we exist in. The stronger the resistance and dissonance we choose, the more walls we construct because creativity within must be used. Understanding that our mental and emotional programs offer us choice and the use of our creative will to navigate our inner and outer world, emphasizes the need for attention to our intentions and the integrity of our choices.

We are co-creative beings living together in the same planet, community, and/or family. We affect one another by the choices we make. When we are affected by the choices of others, we must consider our own choices in how to orchestrate a response for an intentional outcome. The choice within self is always present in every circumstance. Even when we feel helpless or without control, one can choose how to creatively transform the void or the excess in a harmonious way by acknowledging the spark of life we carry at the core of mortality.

We all have wounds and experiences that challenge our desire and will to maintain an open heart. Some wounds heal more quickly than others. Some wounds scar and remain as a reminder of something we have yet to work through. These wounds can feel picked at and reopened when similar circumstances arise to challenge our capacity for creative response. Other wounds remain open, weeping and swelling, demanding our constant attention and increasing our sensitivity to many things, related or unrelated to the wound. This happens because pain demands attention and consumes the mind as a protective measure from further injury.

Vulnerability is experienced when we are concerned with protection of self and protection of our wounds. Vulnerability is also experienced when we seek intimacy and deeper connection with others. How do we navigate the sense of vulnerability effectively to achieve the intimacy we seek in the shared experience of creation when we are wounded? So many programs and rules layer on top of one another with each experience, with each healed or unhealed wound. Our resistance builds walls like a maze that our psyche travels through each day. Is it a sanctuary or a prison? Are the walls full of mirrors or windows? Perhaps neither. Do we lash out at others or lash in at ourselves to prove the will we still have to direct and affect with?

Vulnerability requires a delicate balance of self-protection and open heartedness. It requires open mindedness to new experiences and steady caution while navigating these experiences.

When we embrace the creative spark within and acknowledge our will to direct that passion in a generous way, we must also open our beingness to receive. This mutual exchange is the merit of the experience. The details of giving and receiving may look differently than we expect due to the roles we take on circumstantially. Regardless of these differences, a co-creative spark is motivated and an opportunity to integrate deeper wisdom in healing our wounds for greater intimacy with our self and others manifests. The healing of a wound may require many things by the mind, but the soul only requires acknowledgment of its' creative fire. At the highest degree of intimacy, the heart seeks the reflection of that soulful fire. It is essential to embrace deconstruction as a tool in order to know how to let go of a dream, a belief, and/or a wound. Letting go enables a cathartic release of passion. By deconstructing we learn how to reconstruct and align more intimately the capacity for will, passion, vulnerability, and play that we innately carry in the experience of our sense of mortality and immortality.

....

Creativity may be used in constructive and deconstructive ways within the psyche of self and the choices we make to define, design, and refine the life we experience. The experience of real or metaphorical death can be equally profound. Either engage us to initiate a process of reflection, refinement, and transformation by drawing on the well of inner creativity. We are the architects and the engineers working out the questions and negotiating contracts to build our dreams in order to sustain the sacredness of our body, heart, and mind in the material world. Every relationship, every venture is a choice to seek out, to maintain, to transform, or to release. Our analysis of its purpose, how it serves us, and how we serve it is essential to working out the design. Deconstructing our expectations and hypotheses is a part of perfecting our skillset to utilize the creative force within that is fed by the essence of immortality. Dismantling and discarding all or part of a constructed idea, belief, relationship, or life may be necessary as a path to greater understanding and integration. By doing so, an expanded view for improvement is enabled that inspires the passion to dream and manifest and dream and manifest, etc.

If an individual is in alignment with the dynamic cycles of creation potentiating the forge of passion and directing the strength of will beyond stagnation and catharsis, vulnerability becomes a gentle dance of trust. This trust is founded in the acknowledgment of what animates the soul and the experience of beingness. This is the "something" transformed in every moment enabled by the seed of creativity. It is the origin of all thoughts and emotions. The choice to say "yes" to life and death, as gateways to new opportunities, is the choice to be vulnerable. Life and death open the doorways to intimacy with self and others through the nature of our mammalian imprinting and motivation to understand the experience of existence. Through this perpetuation of "inspire-ation" and acknowledgment of the exchange intimacy gifts to us, the confidence and trust in our own capacity to heal and renew our passions is instilled.

When you are losing morale and your inspiration is waning, seek the reconnection of your creative soul to the engineer of the mind. When you are questioning mortality and feel lost in obscurity, seek the reconnection of your heart and soul to the co-creation of intimacy. Clarify and redesign your art of play and your work of dreams with the eye of the immortal architect.

~ One ~

THE OWL'S BECKONING

They say that owls are the spirit messengers of the night, quiet on the wind, hidden and watching until they want to be seen. Their hoot or screeching call may be calming or startling to any creature in their lofty gaze. The reflection of their magnificent eyes illuminates the wisdom of the unseen. Many cultures associate them to spirits of the dead, loved ones visiting from the other side, or stewards and guides for those seeking the bridge to cross over. Since I was a child, I have had many interactions with owls, captive and wild. Their calm, majestic curiosity and synchronistic presence at times of loved one's passing has always inspired profound respect and gratitude.

When I started to work with hospice patients, the call to be in service to those walking across the threshold had felt imminent for a few years. Working to keep two businesses afloat and going to school full time to finish a Masters in Chinese Medicine pushed my capacity to endure the demands of life. In 2012, one year before finishing my degree, I could not wait anymore to start this journey. The application of my skills as a caregiver and "attuning" the minds and souls of those on the journey of death and transformation felt essential to the future work I would be offering in service to community. Beginning this journey brought so many teachings in life and the process of death. Many attributes in the mental emotional states of others and myself in the roles of caregiver and witness were revealed.

They say that to work with death and the dying is a very special calling and skill. Very few feel confident, desiring, or willing to face loss and death whether it is personal or impersonal. This is true in my experience, over the past 8 years, working in the medical field and witnessing others that I personally know in the final farewells to our loved ones. Acknowledging our mortality and finding peace when loss occurs in one's life requires courage to face the most profound sense of change. It takes an equally profound sense of empowerment to not only endure this change, but to transform our own grief in all its stages to live forward with an open heart. My first hospice patient would be the initial influence in my journey to crack the window open on this wisdom.

In April of 2012, I visited the home of an elderly woman who was approximately the age of my grandmother, 88 years old. Her life had been whole with a long marriage and multiple children. Her legacy was love and connection with a no funny business attitude that strengthened her reserve and her graceful surrender to the end of life. You could feel the love in her home and in her children, who would visit to share all of their possible last moments with her. Her husband had passed a few years back and she was "set on going home to him." Much of my learning about her was through her daughter, who acted as primary caregiver, and the personal photos all around her bedroom. She was positioned to look out the window when she awoke to see the open field and spring flowers blooming on the property.

Due to the weakness of her heart and kidneys she rarely spoke or awakened in the few weeks that I visited to offer her massage and reiki. She would mumble, sigh, and grunt occasionally as her body slowly expired and her breathing cycles elongated. I recall seeing her the day before she passed. The energy in the room around her was radiating, like she was already lifting out of her vessel. The image of her husband's gaze from his photo felt much more intense and alert. I asked her daughter to turn on the radio hearing the call for music. A piano tune played immediately, and her daughter began to connect how much the piano meant to her mother. How she would play often and that she would miss the sound of it. The song was timeless, a romance tune about returning to love. Her daughter and I both felt the tears wet our eyes as we exchanged our gratitude for this woman in all her maternal and feminine essence. My heart swelled with deep humility and honor at being able to bear witness and tend to this soul. Her life was fulfilled and she had made love her legacy.

When I left that day, I reflected in the impending loss of my grandmother on my father's side. Intuitively, I knew she would be the first to go in our family and that this moment was key to remember when she did. It was two years later in December of 2014 that my Grandma Chris would pass at the age of 91. The echo of this first hospice patient and her family paralleled the legacy of powerful and kind elders like Grandma Chris. It resonated with truth about devotion in love.

~Devotion~

Devotion is loving dedication. Honest, intentional, realistic devotion maintains the intent to support one another in the context of a changing world and a changing relationship within that world. The old adage "Nothing stays the same" is directly relevant to any individual who holds sacred the ideology that devotion in love means your agreements and roles are only and forever the same as when you entered the agreement. Devotion in love as an agreement is not binding because devotion is something you create and re-create through exchange with yourself and with someone else. Devotion to self is as important in a relationship as one's devotion to another and for the relationship.

To offer loving support, encouragement, or celebration of another is a code of devotion. This offering brings honor and value to the path every individual is working out and deciding upon in their progression through life and the transformation of death. Unconditional love and support are consistent when the acceptance that the one supporting the other is not in control of that person's choices or the outcomes from those choices. It also offers the kind of support that comes without demand or control of the other person to be or choose what another wants, of and for them. The place where this conditionality is most easily witnessed is in the closest relationships one shares. Partners, children, lovers, family, and best friends, in this order respectively, each create an opportunity to assess and apply one's principles of conditional and unconditional love. It is human nature to subconsciously presume that these types of relationships are extensions of ourselves or dictate our thoughts and actions around principles for how we perceive connection, life, and death. The cause and effect of conditional love is that it begets more conditional love. The question remains: Does conditional love create true respect and devotion for another or is it only the illusion of respect dictated by the framework of agreements that demand dedication and respect? How can one offer and receive respect without demanding or needing to control the agreement?

Conditional love creates protective boundaries from certain undesired experiences that unconditional love does not. Yet, unconditional love is the seed of one's deepest desires to be valued beyond all reason. It is the foundation of perpetuating connection with others so that we are not alone or pushed to the "me against the world" cynicism that is devoid of feeling loved and valued by others. Unconditional love provides a doorway in our confined experiences of the analytical machine we call "mind". It softens the fortress one builds around oneself as they create more and more conditions throughout life, upon themselves, and others. This doorway is the one we as children walk through and children remind us of. Unconditional love is a natural experience until defined otherwise by perceptions in the mind. The perceptions one develops may block or create opportunity to refine solutions in the tidal flow of circumstances and how we manifest our ideals of connection in life.

When the terminal of diagnosis opens to death, the compulsion to seek or offer forgiveness, resolve, and release are related to the call of unconditional love within. The expansion of the mind and heart naturally move toward detachment and absolution of conditions that life has instilled. If an individual is stuck in the prison of guilt, resentment, or regret the release of conditions and values they established in life will affect their surrender for peace as they navigate deeper into the shadows of existence. This refusal to seek peace and resolve may unfold in ways unknown to those living, as karmic cycles, in generational DNA strands and the stories passed on in memory. The legacy of our identity, our failures and successes, and our innate gifts to the web of those we love and share the world with, reverberate through the voices of those who remember us. This ripple effect creates allies for dissonance and allies for harmonic change because of the way we, as humans, learn and become attached to stories we witness or are told. Understanding the power of conditional and unconditional love enables the experience of devotion to self and others, as well as the return of that devotion in times of change and transformation. Stories of devotion in love ripple out into time far beyond one's material achievements in life and the knell of their death. Embracing love and connection can also empower the acceptance of change, transition, and transformation in times of hardship, loss, and death.

~ Two ~

A LION, A MOUSE, OR A
BUFFALO?

"Nothing can happen that is bigger than I am." That was the reading on a copper plaque above one of my most memorable hospice patient's beds. She had cared for her husband, who died beneath the same plaque a few years earlier. Both were in their late 70's and both exited by way of cancer taking over their bodies. She told me their life story as I tended her weakened flesh. Her spirit shined robustly with love and confidence. This was a woman who took what life offered beside her husband of the same ilk. A woman that trusted in her own ability, no matter the pain and suffering of her body and mind. She told me the secret was faith, faith in oneself and the perseverance to manage and make the best of the darkest of times.

This reflection came to me in the second year of hospice care. The intensity of the past three years, working through the demands and illusions of an abusive partner turned stalker, had challenged me to consider my mortality, re-assess my dreams, and how I create with others in my personal relationships. The continuity of this one statement has been with me ever since. It reminds me to acknowledge my own will to power and diligence for choices that best serve my integrity and intentional way of living through each big change on the horizon. The last time I saw her was one week before my father had a stroke. She passed while I was home taking care of him with my family. It was a quiet sweet death, I was told. The slow drift in spirit from body is one of the main benefits of hospice that supports the dying and the family witnessing their loved one expire.

~Learning Empowered Humility~

My experience with this woman revealed an understanding about empowered humility. Empowered humility is the awareness of one's own power within and the capacity to respond to any aspect of life. The cultivation of strength and temperance supports successful outcomes that align self with a shared sense of power in creation. This face of humility invites one to consider creative solutions that benefit self and others without the need for submission or dominion. Empowering oneself to achieve a sense of purpose in each endeavor of the life we lead encourages the manifestation of growth through learning how to wield and share our power with others. Empowering others through recognition and allowing the opportunity for shared endeavors and therefore outcomes is an act of applied humility. In this way we do not rely on others to give us power nor do we hold power over anyone else.

Empowered humility engages us to listen to what we are not hearing when a situation is not working the way we idealized. It calms the cycling of the mind when one's focus is only on the power loss or power gain of a conflict that arises. Receptivity is an extension in the awareness state of humility. When one is receptive, objectively and subjectively, one can be empowered with clarity and create opportunity for shared power. Attention to self is key to accountability and assessing how we could approach conflict differently to have more productive outcomes.

Accountability requires humility and attention to self as a factor in the circumstances we experience. Balanced self-empowerment for creative solutions that support shared power inspires deeper connection with one's personal sense of integrity and enables others to have the same empowerment for their own integrity. This establishes healthy foundations for the integrity of the connection itself, whether it's the connection of self to a desired achievement, a project with others, or the pursuit of sustainable relationships with family, friends, and lovers.

~ Three ~

THE TURTLE & THE HARE

The day my father's stroke occurred I was in the city completing my final exams for the spring quarter in Chinese Medicine School. A friend's husband that happened to be at my father's veterinary clinic when it happened was the chosen messenger. I'll never forget how my heart dropped into my feet, but my mind couldn't make them move. The scatter of emotional shock squandered my reality for about five minutes as my friend told me what happened and what hospital they took him to. I grabbed my things, got in my car, and rushed home to get the first flight out to Florida from Oregon. As Spirit would have it, my other closest friend called me as I was driving home. I felt mute but had to push through my shock and tears to tell her what happened. She calmly organized a flight out for me that evening and I am forever grateful for her strength and centered approach to supporting me during the greatest shock of my adult life. This was the moment that forced me to face the reality of my father's mortality. I had to learn to face that, at any time, this person I loved so dearly could be taken. I feared this might be that moment. Even if he didn't die, this might be the moment he would never be the same. His incapacity may mean any number of losses in the ideals of future memories. This could change my whole trajectory for life plans. I could be thrown into the quicksand of depression through this one moment in the experience of loss that would reflect a cascade of losses as each demand for change in all the aspects of life assumes.

I pushed back defiantly with reserve and diligence as I considered all the options to retrain his brain, the treatment frequency and methods, the commitment of my time and efforts for what I was educated to offer. Most of all, my love, my care, and my energy would ensure his restoration alongside my mother and sister. The hours in the airport were like a timeout I couldn't get to the end of quick enough. My plane had a maintenance issue on the connecting flight threatening to delay me overnight and arrive a whole day later instead of the eight hours I had hoped for. By some grace, I was put on a plane eight hours later that would finalize an emotional rollercoaster of waiting to see him for sixteen hours. I just kept thinking, "As long as he lived, we as a family would heal this," because I refused to accept that this was his story or my story.

Luckily, my father is a strong headed survivor and was fully committed to his own regeneration. Three days in the hospital with paralysis in the right side of his body and loss of speech and this man refused to stay. He even refused to let anyone help him up the stairs when he arrived home and pushed himself to climb them with only my mother spotting him from the risk of falling to a tile floor. My sister and I were unable to be there during this feat, but I recall how angry we were at this seeming irrationality. Later, we would all laugh with incredulity and celebrate the strength and determination of this man we look up to and appreciate for all his displays of ambition and endurance.

As I reflect in the pace of his recovery and the mindset of loss and change, I see how the merit of planning for the future and coordinating goals is essential. After the first week of being home, he set a goal to return to work within thirty days, at least part time. My family and I balked a bit at this need to stress himself out for the sake of work, but it was more than that. It was about purpose and fulfilling his sense of service and reward that would fortify his ambition to recover and restore his capacity to meet the demands of his very full life. Over months of weekly care from different modalities and my traveling home once a month for long weekends to treat and assess him, he achieved almost total physical recovery. His speech returned and his gait had mostly restored, except when he grew tired. My father's push for progress in his abilities to regenerate was a magnification of the mindset "Nothing can happen to me that is bigger than I am."

~ Perseverance, Confidence and Motivation~

Witnessing my father's determination for independence and the regain of function to continue fulfilling his sense of purpose in life revealed passionate wisdom in the relationship of confidence and motivation. Confidence and motivation are essential components of progress for the self and for community. The dynamic use of creativity with confidence and motivation to achieve a goal expands the opportunities one has in life and shares with others. The motivation for introspection combined with the confidence one holds in their personal perceptions and capabilities, directly relates to the sense of motivation and confidence one feels when aspiring to achieve. It is the introspection, to deepen our awareness that is paramount in building the foundations of confidence and restoring the reservoir of motivation during times of ease and times of hardship. Confidence and motivation fuel one another inter-dependently, generating a sustained effectiveness to one's endeavors.

Every day, every failed endeavor, and every successful endeavor may be utilized as a doorway to invite the motivation within in order to refine one's strategies and to progress into something one aspires to. One must watch out for preconceived convictions and confirmation bias where the intent to demotivate or subdue confidence may be limiting. Seeking power beyond these detracting thought-forms, imprinted by previous experiences, requires openness to resetting that bias. Learning and revising strategy, after affirming attention and openness, is the next stage of learning how to access opportunities.

Opportunity is like a chariot carrying one toward the healthy perpetuation of confidence and motivation. When one does not see opportunity even in its simple forms, one is blinded by bias to the existence of opportunity in circumstances that present more complex forms and offerings. A keen eye may see a multitude of opportunities in one moment, while those who do not look at all cannot expect to see. Tides of success and failure flow in and out of individual lives and societies, holistically. The opportunity to progress is ignited by intentional motivation and empowered by the healthy confidence in our will to achieve. It is a perpetual rhythm in the breath of existence to aspire and endeavor.

~ Four ~

A NEW ROSE IN THE GARDEN

There is something special about letting your elders go after they have lived a full life that displayed many rewards and accomplishments beyond their hardship. It's as if you are releasing them from further toil and the gradual perpetuating experience of losing their friends and loved ones, as well as their physical and mental function. Grandma Chris had been in and out of the hospital and rehabilitation centers for near death experiences and injuries over the six years before her departure. She had degenerated into a wheelchair and become blind. She lived with the pain of shingles along her spine for four years. Often, when she was coming to from one of her frequent naps or nodding out, she would remind us all that "this is just existing, not living." Her mental faculties were fairly sharp until the year she began to transition. She would always ask me about things we had discussed in recent or past conversations. Her memory recall was like a vault of details and I soaked up every story I could about her and my grandfather's life. Her final heart attack came after an uncontrollable cycle of arrhythmia. She passed abruptly after being taken to the hospital on the early morning of December 22, 2014. I found the date auspicious, in alignment with the winter solstice; the darkest day of the year that signals the return of the light.

We buried Grandma Chris on December 26, 2014. I remember my Grandpa Ted being very upset that it was not sooner. My grandpa was Jewish. When honoring Jewish tradition, a wake is held for viewing the dead before they are interned within three days of their passing to honor the doorway of the spirit crossing into the underworld. I found his insistence on this ritualistic requirement to be remarkably about himself and his own wishes. Grandma Chris was in fact Catholic, not Jewish, and there had been various disagreements and sacrifices throughout their relationship when their religious beliefs were on the table. I wondered if he was honoring her now in the way she requested. I did not ask out of deep respect for my grandfather and his grieving process, but the concern has stuck with me. Grief is a very powerful emotion. It skews our clarity and shifts our rationale. I felt sure of this after my grandfather sat through the speech from the only pastor available that day to lead the ceremony and decided he wanted this pastor for his own funeral.

The rest of the family, including myself, were insulted by this pastor's mediocre offerings about Grandma Chris and his strong focus on himself. It felt like he did not care about presenting any of the things we had told him about her and her life. He was using the pulpit as a promotional tool for himself and what he offers the church. Nonetheless, my grandfather put this man on a pedestal because of his role that day regardless of the pastor's poor delivery. I ignored the speech and focused on my loving memories of my grandmother, laying in her gilded white, pink, and gold casket, carved and painted with roses. I felt like her casket really spoke for her, a delicate and enduring woman, who loved her garden and tended to her family as the most important thing in her life. Her casket spoke to the sweetness of her cakes and cookies she had prepared with my grandpa, day in and day out, for many years in their family owned bakery.

In honor of my grandfather, the family remained silent when it came to criticizing the pastor. Out of respect for his request, we painstakingly accepted the pastor's role to lead my grandfather's funeral eight months later. Had we chosen to forego his request, we would have all been more fulfilled by someone who could really speak to the pains of grief and the letting go of our loved one with words that depicted their embodiment and inspired healing with optimism. Yet, the concern for going against my grandfather's dying wishes for "our sake" felt like an overreach that was not ours to make. So, we sat through another promo commercial about this pastor's own beliefs and recent life events in the church, with little reference to my grandfather or his passing. We learned from the first time though. We shortened the pastor's time to address the congregation and filled it with more personal voices, speaking on memories and well wishes for the head of our family. This way we could honor his last requests and our own desires to feel supported in our grief.

~Expectations Influence Perceptions of Outcomes~

When emotions are high and our expectations for release and fulfillment illuminate a path to closure, it is helpful to remember that many factors play out in any given circumstance. The cultivation of patience, integrity in the way we honor others requests or needs, and flexibility for the achievement of positive outcomes are essential when seeking appreciation with resolve.

The impulse for expectations and ideals is automatic in our experience of the world. In our efforts to create our vision or ideal we define expectations of ourselves, of others, and of the context of our experience. How well we keep our agreements and meet those expectations and how others do or do not, greatly affects our perceptions of the experience. The outcome or continued struggle affects the narrative we carry about ourselves, others, and the event. When one seeks to have an effect to feel fulfilled the concept of control and the conflict of what we have control over arises. Have we assessed the motive of our expectations? Do we need or do we want to have these expectations met? And how much control do we have over the outcome?

Remembering to have compassion for self and others with the understanding that we are all working out the experience of expectations, met and unmet, offers the opportunity to discuss our perceptions of a situation in productive ways. This opportunity to share is essential to letting go of the need to control others or the world around us and to honor the co-creativity we have the power to learn from, heal from, be served by, and achieve with. Learning to recognize the balance of personal authority requires releasing the need for control over others and expectations of others to live by our desires. It is not about having high or low expectations. It is about needs and desires. It is about making requests and communicating those needs and desires to give them a clear opportunity to be met and honored as a "co-creative contract." Many expectations focus on the external world to satisfy something inside oneself. The co-creative contract may be applied directly to conversations and agreements when processing inner conflicts of the ego experience and the deeper center of one's true nature within.

A sense of harmony and subdued suffering is possible when one releases attachment to expectation, by defining what is unnecessary or detrimental in the imprints of experiential outcomes. These factors influence and dictate how one seeks fulfillment in the world. The invitation is to practice less attachment and to be a witness of self, others, and the nature of existence. It is natural to have expectations and attachments. Finding the balance of acting and yielding in our co-creativity is the way to perpetuate dynamic flow beyond the resistance of disappointment and the ebb and flow of our perceived success. This flow opens the opportunity to learn, to expand, to re-define, and re-potentiate in our creation, by the perceptions of our expectations. Expectations have the power to fortify us in productive ways and to impede our progress in confining ways. The perceptions of ourselves, others, and the world are intertwined with the attachments we carry. These attachments affect how we actively or passively engage in the experiences of every day.

~ Five ~

CALLISTO'S ESCAPE TO THE STARS

Every death is different. Some happen like a shockwave that challenges your worldview and shakes your heart until it finally admits how sad and broken it feels. After the shock and disbelief run out, the horror and resistance are still slow to resolve. Once they subside, the anger and immense grief really set in. That is how it felt when one of my closest friends, Angela, died in a tragic motorcycle accident one month after she turned thirty-four. At this point I had already experienced three significant deaths in six months, but they didn't rock me like Angela's did. Even though we had only been close for four years, we had shared and endured so many big moments in our life experiences together. The proof of our bond and loyalty was steadfast. Her lighthearted vigilance really inspired me out of some of the darker critical programming I carried about life and myself. My gratitude was clear in the wake of her loss.

I think the hardest parts about processing her death were that I somehow felt saved by it and responsible for it. I had planned to buy her motorcycle that month. Somehow, I felt that it should have been me that died on it. I had always thought that might be how I would go if I exited this mortal life early and that didn't keep me from wanting the experience of regularly riding one for fun. I wasn't caught up in the tragedy of her short life when she passed. I was upset because I felt like she was an incredible loving light and strong feminine essence in the world. She still had more to offer, more to share. I wasn't comparing myself to her as though I didn't. My rationale in my love and grief and my perceived role as loving protector of those I care about made me think "I should have taken her place." I realized in all this that what was most important is to continue sharing my love and light with the world to honor her and myself. To celebrate her and uphold her example for all that I cherish in her that aligns with me.

Her funerary ceremony was the first I ever managed and planned with the assistance of her other closest friend, Paul. It was clear that her estranged parents would not honor her for who she was, so Paul and I decided we would. At the age of fifteen, she left the congregation of their Evangelical Baptist Church intentionally. She wanted to evolve into the woman she had the capacity to be without someone telling her or shaming her into being someone they wanted her to be. Their ceremony was a basic memoir to her days of childhood with a heavier focus on the family's grief. I'll never forget how insulted I felt for Angela when I realized they only showed photos of her up to the age she had left the church and did not even bring her ashes to the ceremony to be officially honored. When they repeated for the second time that we could save Angela's soul and heal the grief of her family by joining the church and offering donations, I tried to get up and leave. Another dear friend of mine soothed me back into the pew to continue my respect and silence for their preferred manner of grieving. This moment still deeply invokes the feeling of insult when I recall it. This was another significant moment where I found the distortion of loss and grief deferring the opportunity to honor the one lost for who they were, first and foremost.

Paul and I decided to hold ceremony with a large circle of her friends out in the wilderness, in alignment with her spiritual beliefs. Her parents gave us her ashes without resistance. We scattered them to the wind and to the lake after a bonfire of prayers and stories. Some of these stories were light while others were dark, but either way they were honest. We each opened our hearts and authentically grieved our sense of loss. I remember gazing at everyone before beginning the rounds that would give everyone an opportunity to share. I delivered a speech to honor the presence of our grief for the separation we felt from Angela. I thought I would be more nervous or say less than I intended but my voice fully opened. My emotions waited behind the sense of duty, confidence, and authenticity of my intentions to create a safe container for us all to celebrate our love and grieve. The gratitude from others about my leadership offerings was soothing and supportive but after the ceremony I slept long and hard, perhaps like the death I could feel deep inside now fully present and undeniable.

The act of intentional grieving and ceremonial honoring is paramount to the healing process for most of us. Even beyond humans, many animals hold vigil or congregate to acknowledge death in their clan. Some even have elaborate burial rites that make the presumed human hierarchy of sentience questionable. The death of Angela, although intense to process, still carried with it the understanding of transforming the experience of atomic energy, of vitality, entering and leaving the body. The profound emotions offered me even more of that awareness as a witness because of what she meant to me and how connected we are as soul kin. Over time, I grew to accept the loss of her physical presence, but it has taken more time than many other deaths in my life. Even with the twenty-one consecutive deaths that would occur over the next six years, my memories of her and the shock of her loss were a continual hum in the background. I learned to associate living forward with lightheartedness and resilience. This truth is what she magnified within me, in life and now death.

~Engaging Life with an Open Heart~

The power of an open heart catalyzes the opportunity for sharing and receiving abundant fulfillment. On the journey to open one's heart for fulfillment the choice to explore and to create in the world as an individual and in relationship with others increases one's perceptions of vulnerability. Perceptions of joy, ambition, contentment, security, loss, lack of success, disappointment for expectations unmet, and nuances in a perceived lack of control are all part of the experience in this process. Life events that feel traumatic or unsatisfying can influence an individual to shut down and isolate as an effort to defend and protect the perceived parts of self that are being challenged in the face of vulnerability.

At its' core the challenge is an opportunity to deepen into one's understanding of the resistance in order to create more effectively. It may be motivating us to place proper boundary for self and others, or to augment balance where it is lacking, and to question one's perceptions about the fears, disappointment, anger, and righteousness that may be demanding a total shut down, escape, or backlash reaction to the experience of being vulnerable. By deepening one's relationship to the authentic self and empowering trust within, the power to move beyond resistance and to transmute perceived threats is embodied. Then, the trade-off of choosing the path of an open heart and vulnerability may be viewed as the cultivation of resilience.

Resilience is how we survive not only physically but emotionally, mentally, and spiritually. Throughout a life, cultivation of dependence on resilience may become partial and lacking wholeness. Reliance on protecting only the primary parts of self that one perceives as necessity, can divide the intentional focus of cultivating wholeness which enables reliance on all aspects of oneself. This is evident when one component of how an individual creates in life is successful in resilience while others are diminished. Someone can be great at surviving physically, yet low in the reserves of spiritual perseverance. Another can be well developed in mental fortitude when connecting with others and strategizing successful endeavors, yet poor in emotional stamina and empathy when developing personal relationships and embracing the wisdom of the bodily senses.

As the human species advances technologically, the reliance on mental faculties will continue to dominate. Living life from a cerebral, reductionist, and rationalizing foundation severs the sentient cords of feeling, instinct, and intuition that reveal an expansive network of creative skills to meet life's basic demands and denies achievements of growth through function in a holistic way. It is the nature of the mind to seek control, understanding, and affect when exploring the world and chaperoning connection with self and others. It is the nature of the heart to feel affected and to contain the sensory experience of inspiration through a relationship with self and others.

When the perception of vulnerability arises, the compensatory mechanism of defense is a basic imprint of the survival mind. It is the nature of the survival mind to seek control at all costs in the attempt to persist "as is" in the experience of life. Superseding this urge enables a deepening into the experience of the feelings and thoughts associated with the catalyst of vulnerability. This requires the acceptance of change as a versatile teacher and a willingness to refine one's awareness in the context of that change. Engaging the curiosity of the mind to reveal what the heart contains and how to utilize it with resilience is the way to aspiring beyond just surviving into the art of thriving. Thriving requires the intentional cultivation of multifaceted skills in order to maintain integrity with the authentic self. This pursuit of awareness evolves the dynamic of existence.

Choosing to live life with an open heart and trusting in resilience though the experience of vulnerability is an essential skill in this endeavor. The most profound experiences of fulfillment in the human journey reside in the knowing, receiving, and giving of love to self, others, the world, and a higher spiritual power. The teachings of love come in many forms. The beliefs of the individual are reflected in the intensity and frequency of love as it is experienced. It is the mind that chaperones, structures, and defines what has, is, and will be enabled for exchange. No matter the traumas, losses, and unmet expectations of an individual, the potency of love still exists to be received, cultivated, and shared.

The mask of vulnerability sheds its' skin as the layers of the psyche push forth for acknowledgment, illumination, and enlightenment. The most alchemical transformations are activated by the resolve to embrace one's power and to acknowledge the embodiment of love's teachings as the source of that power. This requires the will to receive, the immersion within that container of feeling, and the will to expand the capacity of perceived limitations within. It requires ones' attention to refinement of mental and emotional filters that allow free passage into and out of this rhythmic reservoir of self. The courage to face vulnerability has no root without love to draw upon. The rewards of protecting oneself can feel hollow and draining to achieve without a deeper valuation of purpose for the efforts of thriving in lieu of surviving. Loving oneself, the essence of life, and carrying love for others invigorates and magnifies the experience of success when the call to learn from vulnerability or the perceived need for protection unfolds.

Choosing to live and love with an open heart, requests one's willingness to experience vulnerability and trust in the resilience of one's power to adapt. It requests that we accept change, loss, death, and the challenges to refine meaning in what we think we know of ourselves. The emotional catharsis of the heart is the fire of transmutation that opens the threshold to the psyche's evolution. Lower the gates to your fortress and bridge the gap between heart and mind. Let embodiment inform you and generate the potency to thrive from your authentic core. Dig down into the root and illuminate a path to create, beyond fear, with the brilliance of love and trust.

~ Six ~

REFLECTIONS FROM A
FUNERAL DIRECTOR

Q: What is the most important part of how you counsel families?

A: "Being present, gracious, and accepting of people right where they are. Reminding them that grief is a process for everyone and we each may experience it differently, and it is important to extend grace and love to people to honor where they are. I share this with those preparing their end of life plans and with those in need of service for their loved one they have lost."

Q: What makes the process of funeral arrangements go most smoothly?

A: "When the family unit handling arrangements is agreeable with the deceased's wishes and each other when honoring them."

Q: What are three things families of the deceased do not think about when arranging a funeral?

A: "One, clients are often unaware of all the legal documents that require death certificates to finalize or dissolve the contracts of the deceased."

"Two, many clients do not plan in advance for death and funeral arrangements and then regret not having done so."

"Three, many are unaware of how beneficial it is to plan ahead, for all involved, and utilize a funeral director to finalize loose ends. This causes them to be more caught up in all the requirements of "to do" lists and lose the essence of the moment to honor the loss of their loved one."

Q: What is your perspective on how to work with the death of your own loved ones?

A: "It is always different when you can plan for it. When it is sudden you cannot plan how you are going to respond or have the grace that comes with preparing for that final moment. Even when we understand the path of grief and how to handle it, the more tragic seeming and sudden deaths are reckoned with differently. It is essential to have grace with oneself when struggling to process it no matter what you know or how many deaths you have grieved."

Q: Is it harder or easier to plan and manage the deaths of your friends and family when this is what you do for a living?

A: "It is much harder and more draining, emotionally. Family secrets that are commonly revealed when death occurs are more affecting. I must maintain the same level of absolute integrity no matter how close a loved one is to honor the oath and requirement for secrecy that comes with the role of funeral director."

Q: What are your outlets to stay balanced mentally and emotionally while doing your work in the world?

A: "Journaling is a big one along with being out in nature and staying active. Massage Therapy is comforting and releasing when stress is high, which is daily in this line of work. Prayer and reflection in gratitude, the positive things in life, and the mystery of creation are powerful. One of the most powerful ways to keep balance in my life mentally and emotionally though, is surrounding myself with nourishing people who are supportive and positive even when life is hard."

Q: How do you manage families with differing views on beliefs?

A: "I support them in discussing and resolving it among themselves unless advice or intervention is requested."

Q: Do you recommend mental and emotional counseling for those that have lost someone close to them or are having trouble coping?

A: "No, I do not advise this unless someone requests guidance on whether to do so and then I support them in listening to what they feel would be helpful for them. Every client receives a detailed packet that lists counselors and other supportive information to help them through the grieving and funerary process. The hope is that clients will take the time to read through it. This is not a common offering at all funeral homes. "

Q: How do you respond to the demands of change and loss in life, personally?

A: "I have experienced loss in many ways but not as much to death of loved ones closest to me, yet. You must use the tools you have to persevere. It's not something you think about necessarily. You just do it. It's built into your heart and just flows. It's how one develops through life that helps them collect the tools you need to persevere when change or loss happens."

Q: Do you have any other pearls of wisdom you want to share?
A: "Yes. I am reminded of something my uncle told me when life seemed to be overwhelming and the hard knocks felt like they just kept coming. He told me to take a deep breath and to stop and take a deep breath anytime I felt pushed to a breaking point with myself or someone else. He said the experience of life is like a waffle. Many squares connect into a bigger form. Your mind tells you to eat the whole thing at once. It can be a lot. So, when it is too much, give yourself permission to eat and digest one or a few squares at a time. Eventually you will integrate the pieces inside of you, once again. I have lived by that waffle analogy ever since. I am so thankful for these words of wisdom. They have helped when I struggled to release myself from taking on the burden of responsibility for others or when working out conflicts with others or myself."

To the Funeral Director:

Thank you for sharing and thank you for your service. You are a lantern at the most poignant time of darkness as others experience their own death or the death of a loved one. This is such a noble role and beautiful gift to offer the world.

~ Seven ~

THE RELIABLE FISHERMAN

When the patriarch of a family passes, the ripple effect through time, family roles, perceptions of generational teachings and the influence of that patriarch on the family identity is like the shifting of planetary bodies in orbit when a star burns out. The legacy of light and darkness are an echo for as long as those who can hear it, speak of it, learn from it, and accept its' influence in their lives. The songs, the recipes, the old blankets, and special gifts given, are all mementos that feed the life and spirit of our connection to another who has passed out of physical form.

My Grandpa Ted was a strong patriarch to the Hightman Family. His many aspirations in business, creative hobbies, enjoyment in life, and serving his community saturate my memories and encourage my own understanding in the capacity we have as humans to be and share so much in one lifetime. He was a man who saw many hardships in life, growing up in the Depression Era, living on potatoes and bread, and peddling in the streets with his father. As a young man he took on multiple business endeavors and fighting in World War 2. He was an honest man of opinion. He was as sharp as a tack to the day he passed on. Grandpa was always clear in his discernment for how to apply his efforts and be a loving, supportive, and respectful teacher. I soaked up as many stories of his life as I could in our waning time in order to safeguard the foundational stories of my family's journey, mixed in hardships and successes. Through persecution and great losses, to new beginnings and great strides in the path to achieving fulfillment, we continue to thrive. He and Grandma Chris were a strong unit that exemplified continual lightheartedness, creativity, and devotional companionship. They were married for forty-three years and friends for much longer. They faced many hard times and uplifting experiences mixed with adventure and constructive change for the fulfillment of their own dreams and those of their children.

I still wake up sometimes at 3 a.m. to the smell of coffee and the whisper of their voices. I imagine them watching the sun rise. It was their morning ritual every day. After Grandma Chris crossed the threshold, I could feel my grandfather waning. His sadness for her departure was overwhelming. We spoke often in these last few months. I checked in on him and sought to be a support in his process around whether living on without her was a worthy trade-off to continued connection with his offspring and soon to be delivered great-grandson, Travis Bloom. It was hard for him to decide. At almost 91 years old, he had become more and more isolated over the last ten years caregiving for grandma. He was lonely. Almost all his friends were gone, save for the childhood friend of eighty-two years, whom he spoke with daily. He shared with me his grief, waking in the middle of the night, reaching out for her, and feeling the empty space where she once was. Life without her was a massive step into the unknown and yet he knew much of what he had and what would come. It was the emotional unknown. The separation of companionship and daily connection for that many years intertwined intimately in the challenges and progressions of a life, is the closest in caliber to the void of a lost parent or child. My grandfather was Jewish, but towards the end he became skeptical of his beliefs. His sense of separation was further influenced by this as he deferred the idea of death to the simplistic degradation of ones' body and mind turned to dirt and nothing more.

His broken and yearning heart burst eight months after grandma transitioned, three weeks before his 91st birthday. I called him the day before he left. I could feel his restlessness all week, in my own heart. He had gone to Chicago, IL, the city that made him. He visited his lifetime best friend one last time and greeted his newly born great grandson, the next descendent of the Hightman-Bloom lineage. Our last conversation was very loving and meaningful as he told me about his trip, saying, "I am very tired now, but I am at peace." He told me he was going to sleep for a long time and that he loved me. This is when I knew that he had decided it was time to go and that his sense of fulfillment was complete.

His strength of wisdom and love never ceased to show and be shared. We both expressed our love for the other and I let him go. That night I dreamed Grandma Chris came to pick him up on the shore of their dream home, where they had lived most of their days in Shell Point, FL. I awoke to the smell of coffee at 4 a.m. It was 8 a.m. when I received the phone call that he had been taken to the hospital at 4 a.m. for a massive heart attack and did not make it. I felt the depth of my father's pain as he surrendered to the exodus of his own father and the ripple of realignment within himself, the eldest son, now the leading patriarch of the Hightman Family. I prepared myself to fly in for the burial to be carried out three days, post-mortem. This ritual timing is the practice of Jewish tradition. It was and honor to be there in supportive presence for my father and his siblings as they faced the death of their parent and I said farewell to this very special elder in my life.

~Leading with Integrity and Intention~

The greatest teaching my grandfather offered in our time together was how to lead life with integrity and intention. The path to achieving what we want in life is marked with obstacles that create resistance and problem-solving opportunities. The forks in the road of a journey can challenge one's sense of self. These crossroads may bring us to question the depth of desire one carries to continue the pursuit of living achievements. Diversions from one path to another in that may reveal a choice to sacrifice one's integrity for the sake of winning or in the face of losing. Your alignment with your core truths and the enactment of those beliefs by leading with intention is essential to maintaining integrity with self and with others, regardless of perceived winning or losing. Leading with intention to honor one's integrity and the integrity of others enables self-respect, mutual respect, and healthy foundations for empowering experiential outcomes.

Leading with integrity and intention is essential to feeling empowered in one's choices and upholding self-worth in any circumstance. No matter the outcome of an endeavor, being in alignment with and acting from one's core truths maintains self-trust. Holding clear intentions and returning to these acknowledged intentions, even in the struggle to achieve, is the foundation of how we value our efforts and actions when striving for successful outcomes. If devaluation of intention and efforts prevail, a perceived self-betrayal is inevitable. This self-betrayal may be miniscule or enormous in the narrative of life, but the culmination of many small betrayals will undermine self-trust and self-worth, perhaps even more than one significant betrayal of the self. It all depends on the individual and their alignment to the principles that define their character. It depends on the foundation of one's intentions and integrity throughout a life. Either way, self-trust and self-worth are required in the symbiotic relationship of living with integrity and leading with intention. When the mind is lost in the mire of rationale, the way to center your focus is to return to the core truth of your intention and follow the path of greatest integrity from there. Satisfaction with self is an essential component to the acceptance of any outcome and acceptance supports intentions and actions for better outcomes.

When everything beyond self is silent and removed, how one feels about themselves dictates how one trusts their own integrity and diligence of will to choose between the paths that arise in the external world. If jaded, regaining self-trust and self-worth requires the acknowledgment of an individual's core truths and the alignment with those truths in efforts, actions, and communications. It is best to begin by leading with intention in the smallest tasks and then the greater endeavors. Leading with intention and honoring your integrity is a practice in every moment. Embracing a sustainable path of self-worth and resilience for the challenges of life requires trust and acknowledgment of the truest identity that defines your center of being.

Know thyself, love thyself, and be thyself in the rise of success and the fall of adversity. Seek to learn more than you know of yourself in every journey and outcome in the narrative of your life. Harness the potency of intentional living and perpetuate the sacredness of personal integrity.

~ Eight ~

HONORING BELIEFS ABOUT DEATH

Of the people I have lost to death, very few have had the same beliefs about the finality of life and existence beyond the physical realm we know on Earth. We each have our own belief about what happens when we die. The question remains; how best can we honor a death in our life as a personal loss, as well as the truth that this experience is happening to another? If one chooses to conclude their own view on death and the afterlife, is this dictating how one holds ceremony and ritual for the one who has passed? Or are the feelings, beliefs, and the last rites of the one lost more important than our own desires and methods to finding peace?

This is very important to consider if we seek to honor a being we respect and love because it is their death after all, even if it is our sense of loss lingering to be felt. By honoring the last rites and the beliefs of others in their life and death, we show our gratitude for their existence; knowing that the choice is still theirs to make. We empower the cord that defines our trust and acceptance in their ability to know who they are, what they want, and where they are transcending.

If they are Catholic and you are Atheist, honor them in Catholic ceremony. If they are Buddhist and you are Evangelical Christian, honor them in Buddhist ceremony. If they believe there is nothing after this life but slow deterioration into the cold hard earth, accept their belief as a choice. If they hold deep trust in reincarnation, know that they will return of their own accord in new body. Death may fuel uncertainty when beliefs become questioned or challenged by others in the experience. Philosophies and undefined questions request attention. When we seek bottom lines and finite answers, we attempt to deduce the great mystery into one belief.

Stand back from it all and consider the peace in this great mystery. Feel the calm tide that ebbs and flows at the corner of your consciousness. When you allow all the possibilities to be true for every individual you allow them the opportunity to be empowered when choosing their own paths in life and death. Then, the greater depth of that person's identity is more wholly revealed to you. It is beautiful in its own space-time. It is art in the heart and mind of that creative being charting the waters of illusion and reality, as we all are.

Remembering humility at the time of death for other's beliefs, more than any other time, is the greatest honor one can offer for those leaving us and our loving memories of them. It also reminds us that we are no different in our own exploration and defining of what feels right for us. The ultimate peace in this journey of death resides in the acceptance of the other as whole and beautiful for who they are. We have the power to acknowledge the gifts and teachings they brought into our lives and what they learned in the world that is worth sharing and holding sacred. These acknowledgments may bring a deeper sense of understanding, peace, and gratitude. It brings a quiet reverence and release of burden from resistance to accept them in their own way even if their beliefs are not in accordance with our own.

Letting our differing beliefs get in the way of love and respect in its purest form is the pressure in the pot that keeps us feeling drained and volatile. Finding peace for our own death is where our beliefs most apply, and we naturally want others to value those rites just the same. Death calls in so many emotions and yet a masked emptiness that cares nothing of fulfillment. Each time we lose another to death we are inherently experiencing a death within ourselves. We are faced with an image of our own considerable death to come. That is why the mind becomes a bridge to help analyze, sort, and consolidate the vast feelings seemingly undefined. Yet, the mind can also get in the way of those feelings, shutting them inside and distracting one's attention in multiple layers of questions, concerns, and reasoning. This disconnected bridge begins to allow emotions to be projected through beliefs and thoughts. These fixations may be masquerading and distracting from the deeper catalyst of the emotion and mire the process of finding peace.

Peace is a feeling. It is a calm space where all the emotions are felt and released without clutching or directing these feelings towards someone else or something. The peace we seek is foremost an effort to finding acceptance and resolve for our own mortality. Throughout this revelation and refining we must never forget that the death is not ours. It is the one who has inspired our dance of introspection and they must be honored first.

~ Nine ~

DIA DE LOS MUERTOS & PRAYERS FOR DIVINITY

After six deaths in one year, my contemplation on death and life changes that ripple out from those deaths was infused into my way of moving through the world. Devoted rituals of honoring my grandparents, one of my closest friends, my 18 year old childhood cat, and a childhood friend and maternal figure, was the beginning or end note to every day. The first death in 2014 was Azrael, a crow I was rehabilitating with a fractured wing. The resonance of this small death felt like it had sparked a revolution in my life. This revolution was transforming the act of honoring death as an impersonal witness and caregiver with hospice patients into the very personal act of embracing and transmuting the loss of those that I loved dearly. When would the cycle begin to shift back to an easier pace of loss and change? I continued to tell myself with each death that this one would be the last one for awhile, but they just kept happening without reprieve for more than a handful of months.

I felt called strongly to San Miguel Allende, Mexico to visit a friend in order to share in the festivities of Dia De Los Muertos.

I was enchanted with how an entire culture of people held such high regard for their ancestors and loved ones who crossed over the threshold before them. The radiant honor, illuminated prayers, and open storytelling for all to share and witness was replenishing compared to the mental, emotional dissonance and depressed acts of acknowledgment that keep many in American life from transforming the pain that comes with loss.

From the color of the costumes and candles, to the delicate flowers and altar assemblages, to the offerings of food and special items with each other and for those in the spirit world, the air of complete presence, acceptance, and joy beyond grief was undeniable. A full three day commitment to sit with the memories or conversations with loved ones was like a grand ball that invited a meeting between the living and the dead to dance together once again. An homage was created in every space the eye could see, intentionally. The stewardship of this ceremony was very palpable to me, reflecting my inherent beliefs. As Spirit would have it, the potency of sharing in this festival was ignited all the more deeply before it ever began.

The day I arrived in San Miguel it was dry and sunny. I watched the sun go down over the hills as the shuttle brought me closer to the city. Within an hour of my arrival, I received a call. My other childhood cat of 16 years had a stroke and was at the veterinary emergency clinic. The caregiver told me the details of how he walked into the house and found her, hours before. My transit had impeded any communication. He said she was crying in the kitchen, wobbly and bumping her head into the cabinets because she could not see, until she collapsed, still caterwauling. He didn't know what to do and he didn't want to have my cat euthanized without my consent. After speaking with the veterinarian, it was clear that there was no way to return her back to functional health. The loss of brain function was too much. So, I agreed to have her euthanized to bring her peace. It was the honorable and selfless choice to make.

The shock of this death was immediate. My grief was full to the brim making it hard to not feel guilty for coming on this trip or for not being by her side when she needed me most. It felt like I betrayed her in some way, like I betrayed our relationship and myself. Yet, I also could not ignore the synchronicity of this happening on the exact day that I left to join in the celebration of death in a very supported, communal way. It felt like it was meant to be, but that was not easy to accept. Some deaths are easier to accept than others. Our state of mind and heart, the circumstances surrounding the death, and where we feel stuck about what could have changed are all factors that pressure us to resist or release. Our expectations of others and ourselves are the linchpin to cathartic cycling we must define, in order to diffuse the intensity of the experience and to learn for future applications.

~Revealing Synchronicity in the Role of a Witness~

Every moment is a multidimensional experience with different lenses of perception that shift in correlation to our objective and subjective states of awareness. Some people are wired to perceive the world with a subjective eye, while others embrace a more objective position. Being a witness of self creates an opportunity to learn how to be more of each. It takes a consistent receptivity of the journey into feeling and understanding all emotions, combined with analyzing and questioning our intentions, beliefs, fears, and desires with respect to outcomes. Acknowledging one's choices and accountability in the efforts or acquiescence to affect the world around us is preliminary in the reflection of our conclusions about the patterns of synchrony that persist to be witnessed.

Confirmation bias, conviction bias, and self-fulfilling prophecy are parts of the witnessing experience. That is why it is essential to break the habit of assumption and check in with the imprint of our reactions and urges. One must harness a sustained curiosity in the comparable differences and similarities of each experience. The question of reality or illusion can dictate projections we or others may assert to be accepted or rejected in each circumstance. Projection is a natural part of our effect on life perceptions and choices as we navigate experiential awareness. This means individually as well as collectively, with others. It is up to us to question and define the purpose of these projections in order to cultivate and refine the skills of witnessing. Acknowledging patterns of belief that influence one's reactivity or responsiveness in each situation enables a choice to modify, release, or empower the ways we affect life.

The perceptions of every individual are marked by one's chosen roles in an experience. Roles are chosen regardless of whether they are assigned or happenstance. Each moment a role is taken on is an integrated analysis of how one is perceived, then pressured, or compelled to make a commitment to that role. This is more understandable when one practices the skill of witnessing. Every moment is a trade-off of rewards and consequences. One chooses their role based on the perceptions of these possible outcomes and acts as their own form of "weighted justice" to make the choice. The Judge and the Victim persona originate in the distortions and fixations of subjectively and objectively extreme mindsets combined with oppressive beliefs. These perceptual personas exist in each of us and it is one's choice to move beyond them through the practice of witnessing. The greater discernment of one's own patterns, including self-talk and reactions to the world around them, cultivates a sense of synchrony in the outcome of choices and one's life narrative.

The witnessing of the narratives and experiences of others and the patterns of nature bestows the conceptual possibilities of aligning with different patterns of synchrony to achieve desired outcomes. Learning vicariously in this way offers a balance to the foundational habituation of living by trial and error. Developing discernment beyond the method of trial and error simultaneously disengages the mentality of the Judge and the Victim. This enhances a feeling of connection and alignment with one's capacity to achieve temperance and confidence to affect their own personal narrative.

To be in synchrony and to witness synchronicity in the context of one's experience, defines the skill to align gracefully in strategic choices and acceptance of outcomes. This skill is directly connected to the sense of empowerment and capability one holds to be directive and receptive in their subjective and objective responses. This applies to self-witnessing and being the witness of others. Temperance may be the most valuable guide when sensing the degrees of one's connection to the patterns in life and personal narratives. The psyche is an orb of concentric layers and every layer offers a different lens for the discernment of one's connection and active role in the experience.

~ Ten ~

AMAUNET, GODDESS OF THE NORTH WIND

When my youngest kitty, Amaunet, was diagnosed with aggressive mouth cancer, it was the first time there was little I could do for my pet besides make her comfortable. All my other fur babies had passed of old age and chronic kidney failure. With Amaunet, it was unclear when the right time should be to help her cross over. My indecisiveness was its' own form of suffering. She was a happy playful cat almost to the end, who loved to eat and looked it. She didn't have enough time for her body to waste. I wouldn't let her suffer without eating or feel the constant pain of a syringe from forcing food past the tumor that was growing in the left side of her upper palette. My turmoil was short lived. It was only a month from her diagnosis that she began swiping at her face and rolling around in pain. She had withheld all manner of pain behavior until that final week. Her pain medication just wasn't working. She wanted to eat her wet canned food but would avert herself within minutes of trying and angrily pace around it. My heart was stricken with fear that her suffering was unnecessary. I knew I could stop it at any moment and release her into that timeless sleep of euthanasia. I argued with myself about taking her too soon or too late. There seemed to be no answer that would absolve any unknowns that might bring regret.

I couldn't watch her suffer, not when I knew I could help her step beyond it to the inevitable death that awaited. The day I took her to the VCA Animal Hospital, she had made it a point to snuggle me all morning, to try to show me she still wanted to play with my dog, her best bud, and that she was still herself beyond these moments of pain. These moments did not outweigh the moments of pain anymore though as I watched her pace with frustration that she couldn't stop the thing that was literally gnawing at her face. Her passing was quiet and quick as she stuffed her face in my arms, purring one last time. Her little paws pressed against my skin were so soft. I didn't want to let her go. I wasn't ready but my love for her and honor for her quality of life was greater. I have no regrets. This death was an experience in walking a balanced path for her needs and my wishes for her comfort.

It has never failed to surprise me that as pet owners most find It completely natural to use euthanasia to end suffering when the inevitable death of the body is imminent, yet human deaths are not perceived the same. Why is it so different? Is it only the degree of attachment to our own human mortality that makes the difference? Why do so many prefer to go the lengths of watching someone with aggressive cancers or severe terminal illness die slowly with or without hospice care? When is it pertinent to acknowledge that one's view of death and quality of life has a mismatch when considering their own death, the death of loved ones, or the death of their animals?

~Death with Dignity~

The value we place in life and death with dignity is unmasked when we choose fear of loss over compassionate acceptance for the futility of lingering on through pain until the body finally gives up. The reality of hospice is that it is meant to help soothe and augment the quality of the ending life, yet many of the practices prolong it to some degree. Choosing to relieve one's suffering or the suffering of others, when they have the capacity to communicate this request as their dying rites, should be considered an act of freedom by law and a way of honoring death with dignity for those we love most. Yet only eight states in the United States have laws to allow a compassionate form of self-euthanasia modeled off the first "Death with Dignity Act" from the state of Oregon. After witnessing the amount of death in my working and personal life it is clear that humans are the closest to their animal natures the closer they are to severe pain and death. As conscious beings with advanced medicine and technology, death is still here to accept, eventually. We are not above it, nor are we above the death of others or our beloved pets.

Aligning one's perceptions of how best to honor death as transformation in the phenomenon of existence is essential to expanding the capacity for compassion about the experience of suffering and death of all beings, including the self. It is essential to honoring the choices of others seeking death with dignity to relieve the duration of pain leading them to their inevitable end. Death with dignity should not be denied or rejected on the premise that it is suicide when it is abundantly clear to all involved that it is time and suffering being weighed. Death with dignity is not a new practice. In fact, it is as old as tribal communities in the beginnings of civilization. When it was their time, elders would walk into the woods or the ocean in brave surrender to what was coming. Medicine men and women would offer plant medicines to quicken death when suffering was intensifying in its' lead toward the final breaths. As an evolved society, perhaps it's time to consider how much honor and compassion for death and changes in life we have maintained from this ancestral wisdom.

~ Eleven ~

EMBRACING THE POWER OF GRIEF

The deaths just kept coming. I knew that each one would feel different, yet some part of me thought it would be easier. I thought I would discover some way to not feel the emotions. The emotions are always there. To detach from emotions for a time in our coping in order to find peace and repose may be an important part of processing acceptance. This does not mean that our emotional awareness for what we have detached from will not come flooding back when we are ready to feel. Cutting oneself off from emotions for too long for any experience of loss or change will ripple out in our experiences of life until they are properly integrated. The question of when and how one orients and allows themselves to feel the emotions is how they transform their alignment to grief.

Whether you are Christian, Buddhist, Atheist, or another belief form, we all recognize a cycle and transition in being. The most starkly framed belief structure is the atheistic "ashes to ashes, dust to dust"- resources recycling back into the earth as compostable matter that feeds life and is still a part of creation.

When we look at this differently, we may see a beautiful depiction of light returned to the solar system as atoms coalescing and recreating together. It is not truly stark at all. All life forms have animation and special characteristics. This is the ambient source of life, always cycling. Death is an absence of the form we want to see. It is a transformation. Therefore, our emotional servitude holds the ability to evolve and transform with our attributed understanding and acknowledgment when it is most applicable in times of loss, suffering, and death.

The stages of grief are real and will flow when answered to, yet one does not have to be overwhelmed by the undertow if they actualize this current of truth in their belief system. I am not saying you will be free of pain and grief. I am defining the balance between attachment and detachment and the power of knowing that calms the aching cycling parts of our experience of loss. Even when many losses or deaths happen in succession over a short period of time, our will to live on for today in the creative forces we feel and share with others may still be found. Our acknowledgment of life and death as an ongoing transformational process can empower and clarify the path through the stages of grief. On a simplified level, every major loss, disappointment, and death challenges us with a choice deep within. It is a choice to stay open to love, healing, and the mystery of beingness or to shut down and isolate from any subject that challenges us to face our vulnerability.

Finding your center within the duality of mind and life during intense emotional events that challenge beliefs, rationale, and the will to choose must occur in order to sustain resilience for momentum and refine clarity for resolve when processing the stages of grief. The divergence from one thought or one experience makes possible the perception of many other layers in our thoughts and experiences. The complexity of perceptions inspired beyond this duality can lead one down many rabbit holes of rationale. Finding and returning to one's center of truth in the tug of war that duality and perceptual constructions create in the mind is essential to maintaining a sense of balance. This applies in times of change and events that challenge one's inherent structures of belief.

If duality is a base design of thought and experience, like light and shadow, or sound and silence, how did the perception of accuracy in one's alignment to right and wrong come about? Perhaps the narrative of religion defines this, or the laws declared by culture and society, are the origin of distinction. Perhaps, it is inherent in the construct of the brain's evolution and grasped through the process of mindful awareness. It seems that "right versus wrong" is far more conditional and easily manipulated by the perceptions of the mind, in contrast to the neutral duality of the experiential light, shadow, sound, and silence. To be conditional in one's mental rationale is paralleled by the dual opportunity to be unconditional; to judge or not judge, to have attachment to an idea or belief versus detachment to an idea or belief. The point is that the true patterns of duality in existence are inherently neutral unless the perception of right or wrong and acceptable or unacceptable is applied to them. They are as inevitable as life and death, regardless of how one feels about it.

The tug of war within spurs us to choose each fork in the road on the paths we walk. The imprints of outside voices and events can be overwhelming and obscuring of our own true nature, especially when many are living from the assumed conditionality of right versus wrong. The most graceful way to quiet the noise outside or within is to release attachment to the experiences during one's inner conflict long enough to ask the questions of one's knowing heart and bodily instinct. Does this align with me? How does this belief or thought serve me at this time? How does it serve me in the future? Is this thought or ideal mine or someone else's?

Bodily awareness is key when you ask a question to center a sense of duality or confusion. The resonance of feeling sensation in the chest, belly, and head are most common when seeking the uplift of "yes" or the dense pressure of "no." There are times when these sensations occur simultaneously in different parts of the body. When this happens it's ok to acknowledge the answer is inconclusive and ask again at another time. Sometimes our sense of integration and understanding are still digesting and a simplistic yes or no is not currently conducive to that process. More investigation of one's beliefs, ideals, resistance, or ignorance to information may be required for clarity. This is the beautiful journey of expanding conscious awareness. Come into the core of your inner knowing and embrace the cord of truth. Release the pressures of rationale and unify beyond the divisiveness of duality, to listen. Seek balance and innovation in service to self and others.

~How Fear and Love Affect Free Will~

Free will is a foundational attribute of all higher order beings in the animal kingdom. The resonance of consciousness paired with mobile limbs creates an opportunity to choose how to direct our abilities physically in the needs for survival and the desires of the heart and mind. The instinctual duality of fear and love is innate to the processes of our interpretations and reactions to the world. These interpretations program our responses to the world as safe or unsafe and nourishing or detrimental. These programs reflect in the perceptions of our choices as effective or ineffective. Free will is the wild card we carry in the face of any fatalistic belief or experience that incites a feeling of powerlessness. Free will is what makes us autonomous in our hearts and minds, no matter the circumstances of our physical being. To disregard one's free will is to become a slave or a martyr to an experience, a person, or a society. The concept of being born free has merit no matter your race, country of origin, or childhood narrative. The concepts of fear and love within one's perceptions of the world are what hold the power to confine and disregard free will or to activate and pursue it. All the layers of experience one records from the youngest age, along with climactic moments of reckoning, throughout life, create structures of belief. These beliefs define ones' capacity to make choices and shift the paradigm of ones' foundation. Honoring sovereignty by harnessing free will motivates one to envision and embrace new opportunities for success.

Fear is a basic instinct, yet in the mind it may be cultivated as an irrational response. Once the analysis of an experience is rationalized, the persistent cycling of a rationale can cause the perception of fear to assert itself in circumstances that are irrelevant to the initial association of fear. If one sees the world through a lens of fear it is a natural reflex to contract away or to destroy the triggering factor in order to "get away." If this perception and behavior perpetuates, it will result in strict limitations on the observance and enactment of one's own free will. Being open to an experience or shutting down to an experience are the most basic responses we have in life. The more we shutdown from experience due to fear, the more we enslave and martyr ourselves to our perceived limitations. The more we open to experience and learn how to navigate our use of free will in choice, the more we expand our perceived limitations and allow the possibilities of what we seek and welcome in to succeed. In the mind, each hemisphere represents this duality of possibility. When cultivated, both offer the tools to be more conscientious in order to change our world, beginning with our choices and the narrative we live by. The left hemisphere is calculating, coordinating, and structuring. The right hemisphere is imaginative, "sensory feelingness", and abstract in its' associative processing. Both are required for holistic interpretation and meaning. Both are required in the act of free will and the choice to redefine meaning and importance in our perceptions.

In brain development and evolution, the reptilian hindbrain or brainstem coordinates all the basic functions of survival. It communicates with memory banks to associate fear driven responses. The mammalian brain or limbic system associates the experiences of connection, sensuality, and emotional impulses. These developmental imprints cultivate family dynamics and social interactions as another aspect of survival that expands the capacity of our species to create together. The prefrontal lobes and cortex, also called the executive brain, is evolving currently and interconnecting many pathways for consciousness and self-awareness. This aspect of the brain enables one to separate the imprinted patterns and base functions of the mammalian (love compelled) and reptilian (fear driven) brain regions. The executive brain increases the capacity for choice and free will through understanding how our drives and perceptions of self benefit or challenge us. Here we carry the key to unlocking the greatest powers of the mind that are innate to our genome, as well as the keys to directing the expansion of our evolution as conscious beings beyond what we know of ourselves.

The initial drive of the will is to survive. The secondary impulse of the will is to connect with others and nourish oneself with pleasure and contentment. The tertiary invitation of will is to define and design experiences that bring wonder, mindfulness, and the expansion of perception and communication in order to act with intention. Accessing and utilizing the power of the mind beyond inherent drives and impulses requires responsibility and accountability. It is essential to weigh the balance of how programmed needs and wants are influencing our sense of free will. Our choices define the narrative we perceive as our life. If one responds with fear most often, the reactionary choices depict a life of many struggles with the sense of aloneness, based in survival mode. This brain loop can perpetuate after one or multiple traumatic experiences or from the perception of challenges in life we feel "are dealt to us." The "dealt to us" perception is a thin line. It can inspire us to work harder to enact free will or push us into beliefs of helpless victimization or ineffectual apathy.

If one responds with love most often, the responsive choice can portray a life of vulnerability mixed with feelings of appreciation, connection and support with others. A sense of struggle, being taken advantage of, and rejection can also result from an imbalance in how we navigate vulnerability. The truth about vulnerability is that it is inevitable. Whether one is fighting for survival in the physical or mental arenas or struggling for connection, identification, and the reciprocation of love from others, vulnerability is a perception of the executive mind as it begins to sort out the balance of needs and wants. Discovering and aligning a healthy balance in how love and fear inform us, creates greater opportunity to form structures of mindfulness and understanding in the experience of one's personal narrative. This power of awareness and choice opens the doorway to evolving the capacity of our species and our interactions in the world we inhabit. The power of free will succeeds when applied to how one recognizes and responds to internal beliefs and events in the external world.

The power of free will exists in the depths of our understanding that experiences are perceived and influenced by imprinted programs. These subconscious programs compel us to react with fear or respond with love. By choosing love and compassion for others or ourselves, the opportunities for fulfillment in life, beyond the challenges to connect and the battles to survive become inherent in the design of the experiences we define our life to be about. If you are here to have an experience of your own free will, how do you want your free will to serve you? Are you wired for fear or are you wired for love? How can you refine the balance of the way love and fear are informing you?

Conscious awareness of the biological and perceptual components of how one enacts their will, in each circumstance, is essential to harnessing the potency of one's free will. There are many faces of individual will including but not limited to, the will within to endure and overcome, the will within to suffer and resist, the will within to open, receive and share oneself, the will within to create as an individual and in community, and the will within to heal from internal and external conflict by refining the perceptions we carry about life and self. Even the choice to surrender is a willful act.

Surrender to the journey of life and cultivate trust in your own free will. Seek the potency of an open heart beyond fear and embrace the keys within to redefine the limits of your perceived path.

~ Twelve ~

COMING TO TERMS WITH THE FALLIBILITY OF THE MEDICAL FIELD

Grief, anger, and regret can feel like a perpetual cycle of emotion when processing deaths we perceive as preventable. It is common to tell oneself things could have turned out differently, if someone or you would have noticed something amiss, or made a different choice that would have changed the outcome in the life of another. Sometimes we try to put ourselves in the other being's place by thinking out, planning retroactively, and bargaining with the experience of sadness, loss, blame, and idealism. Acceptance as a resolution seems too simple and impertinent. Sometimes it is yet, becomes the only way we have left to honor that death has happened for someone we love while we live on.

In the winter of 2016, one of my closest friends in Oregon was due for a liver transplant. He was an uncle like figure in my life, having offered support and many late evenings filled with advice. He was a generous man to his family and community. The liver transplant went smoothly just after Thanksgiving, but

Stevo did not heal well. His vitals continued to wane as they cared for him in the hospital saying, "Sometimes it takes longer for the organ to take on its' expected functions." Two months later, they diagnosed him with sepsis. His whole body was toxic due to a ravaging bacterial infection called Aspergillosis the healthcare team had missed. By the time they diagnosed him, Stevo was actively beginning to die. It was time to bring him home and let him spend the last days of embodiment with his family and friends in comfort. I remember how hard it was for his wife to help him understand that he wasn't going to get better, that nothing else could be done. The infection and the medication for pain kept him mostly unconscious or lucid. We all came to spend time and share our love and deepest gratitude with him for being a strong part of our lives. When he last closed his eyes, in sleep, he was peaceful and ready. He passed February 6, 2017.

I left for Australia and New Zealand on February 12th. This long awaited trip felt more important than ever to clear my head and heart and to inspire a sense of weightlessness and inspiration for life. One of my travel companions, Scott, was also a dear friend and uncle figure of mine. His wife, Kathy, passed of lung cancer after an eight month battle the year before. He was looking for a similar experience and always wanted to see the beauty of these two countries before he was 65. We planned the trip together with two other friends. Scott's daughter-in-law made certain all his documents were in order and up to date before the trip, including his will and trust.

Two days before the trip he came down with pneumonia. It was a mild case, but because he was a smoker his oxygen levels were too low. They kept him overnight and were concerned about him traveling so he cancelled the trip. Just before the 28 hour flight took off across the Pacific, he told me he was bummed he couldn't go this time but to rain check him for the next trip to Scotland and Ireland. He told me that he felt good overall, no major concerns with the hospital stay, and urged me to go and have fun. I promised to send photos and visit when I returned. Three days later, I received the call from his daughter-in-law telling me Scott had passed of a spontaneous stroke. It didn't seem to make sense. We recounted his symptoms and the hospital management. The night of his stroke he complained of headache and numb tingling in his jaw, but all his vitals were good and he was being discharged in the morning. No one checked on him again that night. They found him cold in the morning. The cause of death was a suspected blood clot in the carotid artery. Primary symptoms for a carotid artery blockage are jaw numbness and headache. What could be done now? Scott was gone at 64 years old. He wasn't ready either.

When I hung up the phone on February 17, 2017, the anger of injustice swept through with the grief of losing another dear friend in my life. I heard Scott singing the Beatles song "When I'm 64", in my head and tears of gratitude mixed with pain came flooding out. I was still in the airport in Cairns waiting on a flight to Melbourne. I thought about the "what if's". What if he knew and didn't tell anyone how bad he was feeling? What if the nurses had done a more thorough assessment? What if Scott had come on this trip and it happened in transit, making it my responsibility to get his body or ashes home? What if Scott had not updated his will and trust prior to the intended trip?

I knew there was nothing more I could do now but continue to soak up this journey, in these miraculous landscapes, in honor of Scott's spirit. The next day, I was passing a construction site in the stage of concrete forms and rebar posting. This was Scott's trade as a foreman most of his life. A giant rainbow appeared as I walked by. It seemed to end in the concrete forms. A van nearby said, "Smile, you're on camera" and a restaurant adjacent to it was "Scott's Place". I laughed and opened my heart to this sweet visitation from my friend and began to let go of the injustice I felt for his death. The flow of acceptance that all things were in their right place, even those deaths that seemed preventable, were still perhaps fated. Whether fated or chosen, they were the endnote to a personal narrative, and they were forgivable.

The ultimacy of death is never one moment. The series of choices we make in our life and body, every day, spin the story of our departure. The timing of death is highly relevant to the bargains we make between fate and free will. As a loved one is lost, those left behind may get caught up in bargaining as an act of resistance for the story of the one who's life transformed, we cannot change. What is left is the impetus and the teaching for us to focus on and the stories woven in our own life that we do have the power to change.

~ Thirteen ~

THE WHEEL AND THE CHARIOT

We all have stories of personal struggle through life change, loss, and death. While writing this book, I had a patient who was willing to offer their story on a long road of hardship through dramatic losses and demanding changes. From losing her first close relative to cancer, to being shocked over the irreparable grief of a brother's murder four years after, the demands for managing emotional experiences within and meeting the requirements of everyday life were challenging. When her brother was murdered, her role as protector, caregiver, and supporter was stretched in every way. Her parents were in shock, consumed by their grief, and unable to fight for justice for their son. This woman had children of her own to raise and care for, to be an example for. She took on the court case to fight for justice the authorities lacked interest in. They gave the unremorseful suspect five years in prison with five years of probation.

Forgiveness is still hard, but there was absolutely no compassion for the murderer during the four year ordeal of mismanaged evidence, lies, and the redirected outcome. She reflected in the memory on that day in court for the suspect's final sentencing. The Pope had been shot the same day. She recalled the example he offered the world by visiting the suspect and offering forgiveness, a forgiveness she could not bring herself to offer. During the multi-year proceedings in court she lost her mother to cancer. Her mother's inability to even hear her son's name out loud, to the day she died, was heartbreaking. It felt like one more injustice.

This resilient woman knew she needed to find a voice around her grief and resentment. She felt silenced by her mother's disassociation and did not want to disrespect her. Her eldest son would ask about his uncle from time to time and she did not avoid his questions. "Kids need to be able to ask questions, to understand, and to learn how to grieve" she said, "especially, when memories come up as they age and have more tools to ask those questions." They were hard to answer sometimes. The brother's long-term partner wanted no contact and chose to separate herself and her daughter from all family ties with the intention of starting a new life. His partner did not want the constant reminder of the one she lost. This was hard to understand for the steadfast woman's son. Her brother's death brought a tide of loss with it, due to the struggles of other family member's inability to cope with it. This left the woman feeling like the only one willing to honor her brother.

In 2006, a criminal released on parole was out driving 110mph on a joy ride. They crashed into her eldest son, who was driving home from a friend's house, killing him instantly. He was 22 years old. The suspect was given 10 years in prison because there was no evidence indicating intentional harm. Although the media attempted to create a story that would target the justice system and police department's efficacy and practices negatively, their role in the accident was very supportive to her family in the tragedy of the situation. The justice system seemed redeemable this time, in her eyes. When her son died, she said she felt "It was very important to talk about him, to keep his memory alive, and grieve openly with her immediate family." They still watch stupid movies and shoot off fireworks to honor him each year, together. Emotionally, she felt less angry this time, but her sadness is always there in the background.

When her second son was hit directly by a vehicle at 25 years of age, while working on the road in a tractor, she did not lose him completely. The traumatic accident caused massive neurologic damage, reducing his developmental persona to the likeness of a five year old. He was in a coma for two weeks and not expected to live. Multiple surgical interventions took place to help restore his life and functional capacity. She is thankful he is still here to share life with, but the perpetual demand of caregiving requires time for selfcare that is hard to find. The suspect that crashed into him served no time, on the technicality that police had not issued a citation when the accident occurred. A monetary settlement for care did take place, but it took three years and required a lot of pushback for the changing stories of the suspect. In this circumstance, forgiveness is palpable, perhaps because her son is still alive, and the suspect was not a criminal from a legal perspective or history. Her compassion is present every day with her son, but she feels a constant frustration that he will never progress or learn like most people, due to his brain injuries. "Patience is a constant teaching," she says. She is "always on watch to ensure he is ok."

In the same month her second son was put in a coma her husband was diagnosed with Parkinson's disease. Over the years, his needs for care and attention have been growing. Her life has become caregiving completely. The mental fatigue and constant place of authority has taxed her reserves and there is no one else and no time for her to reset or create balance in the needs she feels deep within. Putting herself off has become normal, although she does try to take an hour or so every few weeks if she can get it. In 2018, she fell and broke her upper right arm, her dominant side. This forced her to let go, a little, even though she had a fear about being unavailable to make sure everything was taken care of for the family. It was helpful to witness the family support her, in return, and self-manage as best they could to fulfill daily routines. When she realized this, a layer of personal pressure was released. This made it slightly easier to be in her role as caregiver, while honoring her own needs, with less fear when it is essential.

In her wisdom she admitted, "You have to find something just for you- something to fulfill your reserves. If you are angry you must find a way to vent the anger. A soundproof room for yelling it out would be nice. It is powerful to have your tantrum in a safe secluded space. Doing this provides a cathartic release until you are laughing and sobbing with fatigue. You aren't angry anymore then. The pressure feels less and the experience of life feels more acceptable for awhile."

As I reflect in this resilient, compassionate, patient, honest woman's story, the patterns of her narrative resonate. The constant flow of challenges to take on different roles or more intense responsibilities, have required humility, adaptability, and motivation. The will within, to be a part of life, refusing to shut down, and exemplify the principles of devotion are apparent. Although she has felt it is her duty and obligation, that belief is woven in the core of her identity. Is she this way naturally? Or did she choose to continue showing up, no matter how hard life has become?

Every day is a choice to learn something new. Every day is a choice to feel purpose and apply meaning. Every day is a choice to honor the emotions within and simultaneously fulfill the tasks before us. The journey through life is a practice of deepening understanding, letting go, and cultivating stillness to activate the creative power within, in order to feel moments of lightheartedness.

~Resolving Guilt, Resentment, and Regret~

The energy in life required for fulfilling one's endeavors and maintaining innovative solutions for challenges that arise can be stifled by thought and emotion. These emotions and thoughts can create resistance to motivation and to clarity if left unidentified and unresolved. In a world that bases its' conditional beliefs on right versus wrong, the experiences of guilt, resentment, and regret are frequent. The opportunity to process perceptions and re-align one's understanding to release the drain of these foundational beliefs, in order to influence growth with liberating wisdom, is often lacking. The path of growth and liberation requires the application of compassionate communication with self and with others. Guilt, resentment, and regret are negative forms of reinforcement in the mind. They take more than they offer when viewed from a map of possibility in skill development, that engages motivation instead of inertia. While these negative re-enforcers do have the power to promote a sense of empathy for others and conscientiousness of self for one's role or effect in an experience, positive re-enforcers such as seeking understanding, acts of forgiveness, and harmonic resolutions for future similar contexts open the mind and heart to be inspired for different outcomes.

Inspiration naturally invokes a sense of vitality to engage with life, connection with one's endeavors, and with others. Guilt, resentment, and regret imprison the power of motivation and decrease one's self-esteem when it comes to capability, living forward beyond loss, and a healthy balance of accountability with self and others. Guilt, resentment, and regret all originate from the "Judge and Victim" narrative that superimposes itself on an individual's sense of willpower. This is not compassionate communication, which seeks understanding and authenticity of one's intention, without blame or shame, and consults a path to resolution that is chosen with the goal of mutual empowerment. Mutual empowerment enables inspiration to move beyond inertia and to motivate one's will to choose differently for more fulfilling outcomes.

The perception of one's "quality of life" can shift dramatically depending on the view of self as a part of this life. When one feels less capable, less effort is generated in the will to progress or even maintaining life at all. Depression and outrage are common digressions for depleted inspiration, self- esteem, and the will to learn. These digressions are a red flag that our emotions and thoughts imprinted by the experience of "Judge and Victim" roles have welded a sense of entrapment one is resigned to or rebelling against. To resolve depression and outrage, one must seek a new template for perceptual deduction that aligns with the liberation of the "Victim" within and reframes the "Judge" mentality to the role of a "Compassionate Guide." Active refinement of language in how one speaks to themselves is the first step to offering a more compassionate language with others. Examples may be similar to the following:

Judge: "Why are you always messing things up?"
Guide: "What is it that you cannot give yourself? Do you feel worthy?"

Judge: "Why do you have to react like that?"
Guide: "Why did you react? Does your reaction fit the moment? How can you respond instead of react?"

Judge: "You deserve this." "I don't deserve this."
Guide: "Based on your intention, do you deserve this? How can you learn from this outcome? Can you change it now or in the future to have a different, more fulfilling or appeasing outcome for all involved?"

In cultures and families across the world there are varying degrees of unhealthy reinforcement. The age of the individual, family fracturing, and institutional impressions have influenced a learning environment that calls for striving beyond the dissonance in order to achieve the feeling of wholeness in one's mind, heart, and spirit. This call to strive beyond signifies the potential of hierarchical brain development. Humans have been evolving greater use of the prefrontal lobes portion of the brain that have the capacity to shift the focus of the mind to learn vicariously, refine the process of understanding, and to create and choose differently. This means that healing imprints, learned from experiential awareness throughout one's life, is possible and may be used as a tool to purge the binds of guilt, resentment, and regret, or any other stuck emotions one suffers from. In the Patanjali Sutras, a sage is quoted as saying, *"The pain is inevitable the suffering is an option."* Quality of life is sustained and expanded by one's capacity to grasp the teachings and allow thoughts and emotions to inform, from a place of guidance and curiosity, to create more successful outcomes instead of the confining judgments that demand consequential suffering from oneself or others.

The "Compassionate Guide" within may be likened to a merciful god or to a loving parent capable of being fully present as an extension of oneself. Even if the belief in a god or the existence of this benevolent parent is not a part of one's narrative, the desire for this loving embrace and guidance exists in each of us because the "inner child" still lives on as a part of the subconscious self. Guilt is a punishment to the inner child creating a victim experience by self or others and leaves a stigma until resolved. If guilt is left unresolved the stigma deepens, carving out a sense of self-doubt that mires healthy confidence. Resentment is consuming of one's life force, muddles mental emotional clarity, and blocks the path to resolution and closure. When resentment lingers unresolved, it begins to shut down the function of resourceful innovation and creativity, resulting in inertia. This inertia may affect many elements in one's life endeavors. Regrets are the empty shells of unresolved emotion that lack fulfillment in choices made or never embarked upon. The residue of regret can immerse one so deeply that vitality withers and motivation for dreaming forward fades. Regret is a stalemate in the mind that reveals the outcome of an inner conflict that has been given the power to rule one's life and perceptions of self, limiting the experience of self-acknowledgment and gratitude for what one has fulfilled. The more regrets, the less fulfilled one has allowed their self to be.

The re-enforcers that weaken one's ability to preserve vitality, inspiration for fulfillment, and quality of life may be consuming to the point of manifesting disease in the physical body. As vitality wanes in the presence of parasitic emotions and regeneration of inspiration for life endeavors reduces, the body follows suit with the mental emotional directive. In order to perpetuate one's potency of will and openness to life through learning and connection, attention to how one communicates with self and others is essential. When the perceptions of guilt, resentment, and regret arise, the act of choosing to be curious, to understand oneself and others, and to seek liberation through wisdom for creative solutions will lead the way to new paradigms. These new paradigms of thought, emotion, and creative choices, beyond judgment and victimization, override the programs that result in the experiences of suffering and inertia. Embrace your inner child with loving guidance and release limitations binding vitality. Choose compassionate forgiveness to allow receptivity for creative resolve. Seek a quality of life that inspires gratitude and embodies no regrets.

~ Fourteen ~

A HALO OF LOVE AND
GUARDIANSHIP

Animals are the quiet supportive guardians that witness, love, and nourish us through the circumstances of life. They can be like children calling us out of our mental emotional distractions to be active in play and mutual adoration. Some may be our primary companion and friend, the children we never had, or the faithful protector of our home and family. Others may be a spectacle and a curiosity to amuse oneself with. Regardless, their absence is missed when there is true appreciation for what we have shared and experienced with their presence. The closer and longer the devotion between human and animal, the more intense the experience of separation and grief become. When their health declines and the question of how or whether to pursue treatment occurs, beliefs about responsibility, connection, and acceptance for their impending loss arise. Throughout my life I have been the caregiver and companion for many types of animals and walked them across the rainbow bridge when the time for their departure arrived. Every bond was different because of the personality of every being and the circumstances that shifted my experiential awareness around our connection.

There are some animal bonds that stand out strongly more than the rest because of these character differences and time period of life. My Siberian husky, Halo, was one of these. His absence in the physical realm is still felt almost daily, even though he transitioned in 2017 and I have since acquired two new incredible female dogs to be a part of my home and family.

Halo Noksukal was just that, a "Light Warrior." He was my guardian by day and night, the child I never had, and my closest companion through some of the hardest times of my life. He often journeyed with me in my dreams at night beyond the day-to-day travels and adventures in the waking world. He still comes through in my dreams, frequently, as a guardian and a messenger. Halo was more bonded to me than any dog I had ever known before. He spent 12 ½ years with me, from the age of 21 to 33. He was there from the move to Oregon from Florida to build a new life, through an abusive relationship I struggled to understand and relinquish for three years, and intense breakdowns in my physical health after a chemical exposure and major car accident. Through my father's stroke and thirteen deaths in succession between 2014-2017, he witnessed me, loved me, reminded me to keep a light heart, and protected me. One month before his sudden illness, I lost two men in my life that I looked up to within twelve days of each other.

My push to fulfill longstanding desires on my bucket list before my own death might occur, became my way of living. After supporting others, carrying ceremony, and processing so much grief around consecutive deaths, I needed to break free. In early 2017, when I chose to travel to Australia and New Zealand, it was a defining moment of detaching from the fear that I might not be available in the event of crisis for someone I loved. With this journey, I would honor and acknowledge myself for the loving effort and time I had consistently offered to all those I had lost as well as their loved ones that I felt connected to. I needed this time to reset, restore, and feel the freedom of enjoyment without the presence of pressure by anyone or anything for two weeks. It did not come without consequence and further challenges to accept loss and transformation. Just before the trip, I lost my friend Stevo and five days after my departure, I lost my friend Scott. They were both like uncles to me. Approximately 2 ½ weeks after my return, Halo woke me at 2 a.m. panting heavily, whining, and incontinent, before he collapsed. His gum color was rapidly fading as I loaded him in the truck, rushing to the ER. He was barely present when we arrived 40 minutes later. They treated him with steroids, painkillers, and IV fluids. He was diagnosed with a massive hemangioma rupture on the spleen, an aggressive cancer that likely had developed over the past month or so. They had me transport him to Dove Lewis Veterinary Specialists for surgery. The prognosis was poor.

My grief and shock were so intense. I could not decide whether to proceed with surgery or compassionately accept it was his time and help him along with euthanasia. With the size of the hemangioma and the fact that it was a blood cancer, the likelihood of metastasis to the liver and other organs was high. Even if he made it through surgery, I could only get 1-6 months more with him. What was the answer? How could I weigh out such an uncertainty for that amount of time? More than anything I didn't want to let him go. I wasn't ready to release him, to be without him. I didn't know what else was coming in my life and I had so much gratitude for my time with him. In that moment, I could not choose. I felt frozen. I asked my parents to choose for me and we went ahead with surgery. He survived, but with small hemangiomas already proliferating in his liver. He lived for three more months before transitioning on his own at 4:20 a.m. June 12, 2017.

The day he passed out of body was a good day. He was feeling bright, curious, and indulgent. You could see the pain in the pupils of his eyes, but he was determined to track and sniff in the wildflowers on that warm sunny day. He ate well, he played in his own way, and we sunned ourselves together like any normal June day in years past. When we returned home, he curled up on his bed and did not have the desire to get back up. I slept on the couch next to him, as I had those last three months, to attend to him since he could not make it up the stairs. Any stretch on his abdomen would further tumor necrosis in his organs and I knew his push to be active that day was significant. "You can't keep a good dog down", they say. I have nothing but gratitude and joy for the beauty, grace, and wholesomeness of how he wanted to spend his last hours with me.

When I awoke to him crying out a final whimper, I heard the jagged rhythms of his final breaths. I stroked his fur gently, singing and chanting to him that it was ok to go, that I loved him, and that I was so thankful for our time together. Then, he transformed. The warmth of his light left his body but lingered as a halo around me. I cried so many tears I had a headache for days. He is irreplaceable, like so many of us are. He will always be missed, and I will probably always cry when I think of how much I miss him, love him, and have gratitude for our time to-gether. Accepting the potency of this cathartic experience and moment of vulnerability is a gift I cannot deny. It only invites in the opportunity to feel the wisdom in love and connection even more.

Although I couldn't see it yet, Halo's exodus brought with it the message of how strong I had become in my sense of self, roles I take on in the world, how to protect myself in the experiences to come, and how to be reborn again and again from the perceptions of trauma, loss, and death. It also requested of me the question: How to dream forward? Within two days of Halo's transition, my lover's husky also passed of chronic kidney failure caught too late. One day after that, my father ended up in the ICU after a traumatic car accident that collapsed his lungs and fractured his ribs. I had little time to grieve initially, as other demands for caregiving and the anticipation of "what next" took the lead, but I would return again and again over the next two years to this question.

At this point, I began to feel like Chiron ferrying the dead ones I loved across the River of Styx. I had to ask myself, "Is this what my training has been for all along? Was creating offerings for the dead my foundational gift to the world?" I pondered on whether I wanted to do this anymore for anyone and whether to release myself from the role. I had come to a breaking point after showing up, again and again, fighting with love and great effort to maintain that love in the form of gratitude over grief and depression. I hit a wall. It felt like my cup spilled out and all the love I had been using as a healing salve was dull and quiet. I had lost the sense of the Beloved. I could not feel the affection I naturally offer others as total as I once had, and I could not feel the love embracing me. Like a light, I felt burned out. It was unclear what vestige of time, peace, and love I would need to witness, in order to feel the spark inside me again or to restore my once endless fullness.

I felt vulnerable, truly for the first time, in my awakened life. I felt without protection or healing. Love was always my way. Should it not be still? How do I re-embrace and welcome back in the vitality and brilliance of the love I have always counted on to be who I am in the world, to weather the storms of suffering and disappointment? I felt truly submerged beneath the dark cool soils of the earth to rest as though dead like the vessels of the others.... but this is different. This is just existing without attachment or inspiration, without the warmth of passion which I could feel just beyond my reach. My heart and mind were strained from reaching, confused by the inability to get there. My efforts persisted, digging down into the root of my will to discover the desire to dream, to make plans, and to follow through on manifesting dreams renewed.

~ Fifteen ~

A BLOOM SPREADS HER WINGS

Sometimes the message of impending death can feel sudden and shocking, like there is no time to prepare or successful intervention that will lengthen one's life. Terminal illness can be obvious or insidious. Cancer is a mysterious pathology that challenges the will and beliefs of those who are diagnosed and their loved ones. Seeking clarity for how to process all the factors involved, from diagnosis, to treatment, to prognosis, and weighing the options for quantity and quality of life is often overwhelming. Cancer is commonly quiet and slow in the beginning stages. Even the highest stages of metastasis may be unknown until the body can no longer compensate and it begins to waste. The parasitic proliferation of tissue that clogs and diminishes the flow of vitality, corroding the function of organs, brings many layers of hope, doom, and denial to be reckoned with. The signs of ailing health often arrive early on but are passed off as insignificant or contributed to life stress. Lack of self-care, the will to persevere or ignore, and at times, alternate diagnoses of symptoms that fail to acknowledge the root of an ailment can obscure the symptoms of cancer.

Every person differs in their willingness to accept or fight the fate of their own death sentence. The idea of treatment as an offering for last resort opportunities to overcome the sentence of terminality is seductive, no matter how strong an individual is in their acceptance of death. The pressure to stay with loved ones for as long as they can, investing their life savings for no guarantee of days, months, or years, is a carat of gold not easily relinquished. The lack of acceptance and support for their impending death by loved ones clinging to them out of fear and grief for separation heavily influences the mindset and emotional grace one may have the power to cultivate for their own journey across the threshold. In these magnified emotional tides, it can be hard for pragmatism to hold sway but the act of weighing the options for valuation and validation of a choice is an essential part of any major change in life. This is true, most of all, in the transformations and transmutations of the beginnings and endings in embodiment, as we know it.

My Aunt Cindy passed October 22, 2018 of lung cancer. She had a history of asthma and used cigarettes on and off for most of her life. She was diagnosed with COPD, without imaging, approximately one year or less before her cancer diagnosis. By that time, she could barely breath because the tumor in her lung had begun to block the trachea. It was too late. They diagnosed her with small cell carcinoma of the lung three weeks before she transitioned. They offered her all the possible treatments for cancer, even though her body was unlikely to respond. I was surprised when I heard she was planning to accept the course of chemotherapy. She didn't have the time to start it.

Sandra (Cindy) Bloom was an herbalist and a naturalist for most of her life. She honored our Native American heritage by helping the reservations in the Midwest have a voice for their land, rights, and sacred sites. She ensured a place for the lineage of Native wisdom about plant medicine and spirituality in society. She had been clear about her place in the world and honored death from a place of beauty, grace, and synchronicity, for as long as I had known her. There was always the other side of her that was an anxious micromanager. Her opinionated fire called for balance and refuge in the teachings of Native elders. I saw her clinging and hope for the extension of life, as the validation in her devotion as a mother to her children, a partner for her husband, and a caregiver for her family. I saw her exhilaration in the role of "Grammy" to her grandchildren and I saw her fear in leaving them behind.

She was hospitalized 10 days after her diagnosis. It was then that she acknowledged her opportunity had passed. She attempted to prepare her family, knowing it was her time to cross, as the medical team helped her into a hospital bed. After that, she went in and out of consciousness for a week or so. She stirred into consciousness the morning she transitioned, to tell her family "it was time" and that "our ancestors had come" for her. She professed her love for each of them and that she knew they were going to be ok. A red-tailed hawk circled outside her hospital window, the light from its wings shining in the sun, as it rose higher on the thermals that carried it toward the sun.

This story along with the video of the hawk circling in her last moments was shared with me upon her transition. My parents and I had chosen to meet in California to explore the vast mountains and giant Sequoias in Yosemite National Park, as a way of sharing her expected passing. We trusted in our spiritual connection and love in the last exchanges we had with Cindy before she lost consciousness. Sadly, my father lost his cockatiel of twelve years, Snow, the same day as his only sister. I felt protective of him in the weight of grief from these simultaneous deaths, even with his assurance that he would be ok and process them in his own way, in the days to come. I knew my mother would support him and acknowledged, as I have many times, the strength of their companionship and capacity to fulfill multiple roles for one another throughout life's experiences and the demands of emotional introspection that refine our perceptions of self and existence.

Out of the thirteen deaths I experienced and facilitated ceremony for between 2014-2017, I found myself without words and impetus to be a ceremonial role in this one. I recall feeling the shock of her family mixed with surrender to her teachings of wisdom in the way of life and death. The experience of separation and eternal unity was palpably mixed. I wanted to say so much to them and about her as I sat in my chair waiting my turn to speak at her memorial. When the time came it was like my voice box was detached and I was only a big tight ball of feeling. My strength to wade through the emotion and raise my intentional voice was staunchly reversed. I felt ashamed and underserving of her and my family for not standing up to speak but I realized that there just were no words that I could say, better or differently, that would achieve the expression of my love and gratitude for this woman and her influence in my life, in the family, and in so many other lives. She was my grandfather's daughter and she was the closest role model in the Hightman Family Elders to my father.

As I grieved her transformation with sadness and gratitude for all she has shared, I realized that this was one step closer to the probable experience of losing my own mother and father. In this knowing, I released myself from shame or guilt for not having spoken at her memorial and prepared ceremonial bundles for my uncle and cousins in honor of Cindy, to resolve any withstanding need to express my love, appreciation, and acknowledgment of her to them and for them. It has always been my understanding that the path to resolving regret is in the choice for healing and transforming that regret into an expression of wisdom. We may not always be able to get the opportunity or time back that we desire in the circumstances of life, but learning how to creatively move forward, to share what is in our hearts when we find the state of being to open them, and to honor the wisdom in experiences of our past is essential for a sense of fulfillment within our will to choose.

~Remembering How to Dream~

If there is one thing my ancestors have taught me, it is "remembering to dream". Dreaming is how the mind, heart, and soul communicate. Deep longings, playful whims, and hidden messages lay in the fabric of our dreams. Dreaming awakens pieces of the self that serve our creativity in the Now. It is a channel that opens in the meta-conscious states of sleeping or meditating and when you are fully conscious in the waking world. The mind knows how to dream, the heart knows how to dream, the soul knows how to reveal itself through dreams. When the heart or mind are encapsulated by the resistance of blind spots, the overwhelm of un-integrated emotions, or cyclical fixations in thought, dreaming becomes harder to achieve. Extending our efforts to dream may feel like too high a demand in the face of a personal struggle to accept change, loss, and death. The truth my ancestors taught me is that dreaming takes little effort at all, and that stillness and quiet are the allies that enable the gateway of dreaming to re-open.

The call for effort lays in the act of manifestation. When reconstructing the pieces of one's life after great change, loss, or death, we must give ourselves over to the transformation with patience for the many transitions that arise in that journey. In 2018, I held the intention for redesigning the structures of my own life in order to feel purpose and inspiration in the act of creating something new. I purchased property for personal sanctuary and the eventual manifestation of a wellness retreat and sacred community space to share with others. Embracing this journey was a big step in a new direction with many responsibilities and opportunities to learn and to heal the deep wounds of loss. Although death and loss continued to be a strong theme and occurrence in my life, the new investment of focus and energy in the land and around purpose in community felt like a rebirth. It was truly a dream come true and a paramount achievement that nourished the reflections in my spirit and replenished vitality in my heart and mind. It is here that the birds taught me why they sing at dawn.

Remembering to dream provides a balance in the darkest of times. The practices of knowing oneself, facing what feels looming or hidden, and surrendering to the unknown possibilities beyond our calculation of the notable probabilities, grant us new opportunities to manifest forward. Let your mind wander. Give your heart the attention it calls for. Listen to the whispers of your soul and let them teach you how to grasp the essence of your life song. Then, raise your voice and activate that creative zephyr within to follow the many dreams, quietly waiting, in the wellspring of your being. Remembering to dream unveils the threshold of rebirth, again and again, throughout life and death.

~ Sixteen ~

THE BROKEN WEB

It is hard to witness any death in one's life but seeing a loved one waste away from cancer beyond the side effects to cancer treatments available is often one of the most tragic drawn out transformations. There is a bias that arises immediately when one hears the diagnosis of cancer for themselves or for others that they love sharing life with. The prevalence of cancer awareness in society has become one of its' greatest fears and resentments to human life and health.

Most cancer is insidious, quietly growing and taking over functions the body compensates for over and over until resiliency is lost. The innate intelligence of cells that know how to take on new roles in the body and repair damage is a healthy part of evolution unless their codes turn on or off when the body cannot utilize and manage their activity. Like a computer that needs to be defragmented, cancer cells must be sorted and properly destroyed to reset the balance in cellular functions of any area in the body. Depending on the genetics and the lifestyle, every individual will experience this process in degree and pace, differently. Some cancer type diagnoses take over aggressively regardless of the body's capacity for resilience to illness. The questions of "why?" and "how long do I have?" will always be the first to arise. These answers are harder to define than we would like and that only fuels more fear about living and dying. This fear drives conflict in relationships when a diagnosis is dealt and existential thoughts unfold around it or how to treat it. It is natural to want our loved ones to fight and to demand that we, ourselves, fight if the diagnosis belongs to us. It is also natural to acquiesce without regret and make peace when one feels it is their time. This is the catalyst that opens the door to spiritual transformation beyond embodiment.

The medical field exists to rescue, to palliate, and to sometimes cure injury or disease in the body. The assumption of a "magic bullet" to kill any disease, whether pill, infusion, or surgery, is taught to us at a young age. The courage of those that choose to practice medicine is valuable to promoting a healthier, long-lived society. As praise and gratitude should be given to them, there should also be a balance of caution and self-advocacy. In our ideals of medicine, lay the origins of illusion and self-betrayal. Many choose to lean on medicine as the safety net, instead of making healthier choices for body, heart, and mind throughout life. Attitudes toward medicine as a first resort, instead of a last resort, have exponentially expanded health care systems, pharmaceutical defaults, and dependency on an authority outside of oneself that dictates how to live with band-aids for unhealed wounds. These attributes have created less self-accountability and put more pressure on the medical field to be held responsible if interventions fail. Litigious incentives and blame for malpractice influence the attitudes and advice that practitioners give, and in some cases become more about legal liability protection than honest medicine.

The biggest question that supersedes all others when facing a cancer diagnosis, involves assessing the trade-off of quantitative versus qualitative time left in the land of the living. Technological advancements for DNA-specific forms of treatment with greater cellular targeting are on the horizon, but the conversation of what is worth one's time and how they spend it before cancer takes over, returns, or a new cancer develops as possible side effects to previous cancer treatment, remains. After losing four women and two animals in a four year span to cancer, one thing is the same, the very short amount of time they all had regardless of treatment or no treatment. Part of this, is because all their cancers were diagnosed at stage 3 or 4, the most common time the body can no longer compensate enough to hide it.

Frustrations with the medical systems' lack of follow through with patient's earlier complaints and patient's trust that their doctor knew best for them, folded into each story. Oncologists laying out extensive plans for highly expensive treatments that would have short-term effects or none at all, so the patient would know they had other options than consignment to death, provided short-lived rays of hope for the patient and their loved ones. Who can say what is the right decision? No one, but the one who is facing their own death. No matter how hard it is to accept the choices of the one who is asked how they want to live or die and whether buying hope and time is worth it, it is the act of love and humility that reminds loved ones to honor the choice that is not theirs to make. Offerings of support and wisdom, if requested, are the gifts that loved ones can provide as homage to the vitality of the body, heart, mind, and spirit for those standing face to face with their own mortality.

~ Seventeen ~

ALICE AND THE QUEEN OF
HEARTS

The concept of living and dying is an undeniable thought for each of us. Some may prefer to push these thoughts away, to ignore what life and death may mean for them, or how to feel empowered by the existence of life and death. Others lean into it, seeking resolve around regrets, and ensuring all will be taken care of to ease the burden on others once they are gone. Many dabble in a little bit of both and take a less is more approach when grappling with the emotional phases of confronting life and death in the experience of balancing surrender with free will. The emotional regrets in the tides of life circumstances can feel too heavy to endure when we feel time is fleeting. Feelings of entitlement, self-righteousness, and woundedness are a signal that we are carrying resistance around healing and finding closure. Healthy closure provides a positive return to embracing mental, emotional freedom and compassionate wisdom to navigate the path forward without attachments that provoke cycles of unrest.

Cancer may be a short or long road, but either way it is a hard path to walk, in life or toward death. The ravaging of the body by unchecked growth, malnourishment, and bio-chemically influenced perceptions of doom, are not easily understood by the one experiencing it or others witnessing it. This is especially true if there is no medical knowledge for how to assess what and why changes are happening in the body. Every cancer differs and every patient is a diverse environmental platform for the drama that plays out in a cancer diagnosis.

My Aunt Kathy is an example of a person who had a dual experience with a long-term, rare, benign cancer that eventually becomes malignant in later stages. She had three surgeries over eighteen years to remove the tumors and various interventions to prolong the period between regrowth. It is hard to say if any of them were truly effective, given the minimal knowledge of her cancer type. In 2016, the malignancy had begun and there was no more tissue that could be removed in her neck where the primary tumor growth was nested. She was already struggling to swallow normal food due to a lack of enervation and muscle function in one side of her face and throat. She was underweight and becoming more depressed and angrier about what she felt was an injustice to her life. In 2018, she chose an experimental study for a chemotherapy drug, that wasn't specifically for her cancer type, out of desperation. Sadly, she became much worse after this. The cancer migrated to her lumbar spine and possibly to other places undiagnosed. It seemed time had sped up and she wasted away within a year. Her anger, resentment, shame about her appearance, and judgments upon others, pushed her into isolation with her husband, who she demanded be the only one to tend to her. No one else was allowed over, except for the rare moments we all hoped were breakthroughs in her consciousness to feel the love, support, and tending we wanted to offer her.

When she refused hospice care as a rebellion against her own death, her selfishness became undeniable. It was hard to understand because she had the victory of 20 years on cancer. She also had 20 years to consider her death and the way she could plan things to be the least burdensome on others, especially her partner, who she loved dearly. By foregoing hospice, she put a huge expectation on her partner to fulfill everything for her, regardless of his own mental emotional needs or concerns as a 24/7 caregiver. Losing her was an inseparable personal catharsis he had to simultaneously go through, while feeling the pressure of her intense expectations and emotional reactivity.

In the end, this did not go well. She was unwilling to accept death until the last week of her life, but her husband was not prepared to accept it. Cognitive dissonance will appear if we feel under the weight of doubts, attachments, and desires to meet the expectations of the one's we love in our efforts to honor them in life and death. Cognitive dissonance will appear in these most poignant moments if it has not been tended to in time with the soul's needs for contemplation and release. That is why being a healthy caregiver in our personal relationships requires time to self and opportunities to restore one's reserves. This enables us to continue carrying the lantern and the salve of presence for those we love. Even hired caregivers with strong objectivity know that they must take time to replenish and refocus in order to sustain the quality of care required for their patients.

He tried to save her the day she died. He pulled her out of bed awkwardly in his age and physical weakness, put her in the car and drove her to the hospital for some miracle intervention that would not be prescribed. She died somewhere along the way. His turmoil about that day makes it unclear when it happened exactly. Sadly, what is clear, is that he cannot offer himself forgiveness for this and she is no longer here to provide it. The spiritual, mental, and emotional contracts my aunt and uncle made in life reign over his psyche as he still lives and breathes, carrying the shame and the guilt of somehow wronging her or failing her. His desire to be with her is another side of the coin. Living forward is not something he knows quite how to do. The cycle of catharsis and grief continue to prevail, soul contracts incomplete and justice unresolved.

~Soul Contracts and Closure Beyond Grief and Loss~

Throughout life we reveal the elements and identity of who we are and who we share life with. The relationship to ourselves and to others weaves into the fabric of our perceptions and challenges us to acknowledge that our beliefs about others and ourselves dictate the freedom, fulfillment, and security we hold the ability to attain. The binding of beliefs and the lack of awareness in how we create and/or serve attachments to others directly relates to our intensity of and perpetuation of grief or a sense of loss. Reaching a state of closure can be daunting when the maze of one's mind and the perceived contractual obligations to self or others stands in the way.

Soul contracts may be subconscious or conscious agreements with oneself or another made as a negotiated trade off. Every day we think about and act on the agreements made to be a part of one's chosen lifestyle, to surrender to or endure external factors beyond one's control, and to recognize how our roles and actions affect others. Every day we choose to ignore or to face discomfort we feel or to embrace and acknowledge the strength and contentment we have in our experience. Every day we choose to accept or resist the depth of connection one has the capacity to build with family, friends, work, and society.

The agreements with self are the first contracts we make in the world as we unveil the feeling of what we have and have not agreed to in our journey of self-awareness. The agreements with others are secondary contracts that can only be fulfilled to the extent that one can remain true to the contracts with self and the capacity we have to any contract with self and others. This means beyond the idealism of what one wants to be capable of. Unconscious agreements can feel most insidious when it comes to perceived bondage in an agreement to achieve the goal of whatever that contractual agreement dictates. Contractual agreements are defined by thoughts, feelings, and ideals blended with personal principles, abilities, and realistic projections of one's capacity to achieve the desired outcome. Knowing what that desired outcome is, is imperative to completing or absolving the contract and integrating or nullifying its' purpose.

Some contracts are placed on us by others that we have not consciously agreed to. These are the most essential contracts to acknowledge, dissolve, and release. The perception that anyone has power over you or that their demands of you are required to be fulfilled is an illusion. The primary contracts with self will safeguard and clarify what one commands of themselves to assert their own will to break, deny, or dissolve the contracts others place upon them. This includes the conscious secondary agreements one makes with others that oppose one's primary agreements with self.

The perception of bondage to an agreement is based on emotional attachment that is exacerbated by confusion and cyclical tapes in the mind. Grief and loss of connection, in life or death, is a prominent place where arguments with self and the renegotiation of contracts with self or with others are played out. The circumstance of a dissolving relationship or experience in the death of a loved one can be overwhelming and confusing emotionally, driving an individual to hold on to certain contractual agreements that can no longer be fulfilled for the sake of an individual's desire to remain attached to the one lost. Moving beyond grief and loss requires an individual to embrace gratitude for what was shared. This also means acknowledging the change of circumstances around loss as an opportunity to continue in life, with the memories and teachings bestowed, and to find closure in unfulfilled contracts. Finding clarity in the agreements with self, integrating the accomplishments from secondary contracts with the one lost, and releasing residual contracts that were unfulfilled and can no longer be completed without the presence of both individuals, are all a part of seeking closure in order to feel at ease with the new circumstances one finds themselves in.

Experiencing grief and loss for another is an inseparable context for the acknowledgment of self and the opportunity to redefine one's contracts with self and life. Grief and loss show us ourselves because the deepest wells of suffering exist in the attachments of the mind we are faced with and often consumed by. Someone can be in emotional bondage to their self as much as they can be by agreement to another. The way to closure is through autonomy of self. Chosen agreements with self are the primary foundation of how one operates and applies these agreements to move effectively through a life of changing circumstance. Re-negotiating agreements is always an option, for better or worse. One must choose wisely with intentional awareness of their own will and capacity to meet their primary agreements with self and secondary agreements with others. Any soul contract may be accepted or absolved once the clarity of an individual's realistic desire and ability to achieve the purpose of that contract is acknowledged.

When someone has died and is no longer present to demand contract fulfillment or maintain progress toward a desired dream made together, it is time to release oneself of the contract and strengthen contracts with self to live forward. Closure is a step by step, day by day, process of relinquishing attachment. To relinquish attachment and the bondage of contracts to another is not devaluing or denial of love and appreciation. The release of attachment is an act of self-empowerment that transforms the experience of loss, confusion, guilt, shame, and grief by offering an objective view that is realistic to the distance felt between oneself and another. Self-love, nourishment, and release of emotional bondage are all essential for self-empowerment, clarity, and peace in the wake of loss. They are acts of self-acknowledgment for the effort one placed in devotional love, attentiveness, and receptivity to share in the relationship created with another. This is the cycle of love, of exchange, of creativity, and transformation.

~ Eighteen ~

A GHOST IN THE HOUSE, A LIGHT IN THE HEART

Neurologic disorders and early-onset neurodegeneration are an increasingly prominent form of terminal illness in our world today. The slow but visible and audible changes in the behaviors and functions of the ones we once witnessed as highly capable, is tragic and demanding. Caregiving takes on a different meaning with loved ones who are an empty shell or a broken record of their personality traits. Some forms of dementia influence thoughts and behaviors that do not resemble any part of the one we once knew. They are trapped deep in the fold of neurons entangled. It is essential to ask for help from properly trained healthcare providers, seek out support groups to process the confusion and pain of witnessing, and to know when to take time for self, to restore and unwind.

My friend, Alison, was diagnosed with Progressive supranuclear palsy at the age of 50, in 2015. Progressive supranuclear palsy presents like the combination of Parkinson's with Lewy-body Dementia on steroids. Her degeneration took four short years. She passed at home with her husband, one of her daughters, and one of her closest friends on the early morning of February 17, 2019. She was 53, just 1 ½ months shy of her 54th birthday. This may be considered a blessing by those who have tended a loved one with dementia or Parkinson's dIsease for 10-20 years. Regardless of the length in time, watching Alison's quality of life and function plummet to infant status was taxing on all of us who loved her. Staying lighthearted and comedic was our refuge and "Al" preferred it that way, most of the time.

Reasoning with her in the beginning stages of Dementia was impossible as she made riskier choices without the ability to accomplish them safely. Her already petite frame became very frail in two years and the stamina of this community voice, mother of four, and enthusiastic powerhouse in life, became dim and quiet. Even when she could not speak anymore or move her eyes much, her resilient character within told you if she meant "yes" or an adamant "no". Although she moved as slow as a sloth, she would reach out at you when she wanted something and she would hug like a vice with love and appreciation.

In that first two year period, it became clear that she needed 24 hour supervision. Her husband Rob continued to work to support the family. Their kids and friends stepped up to watch, feed, and care for Alison when he couldn't. Their church community created a meal schedule and rotated preparation and delivery of pre-cooked meals. That kind of support is uncommon, but it is possible when one learns to ask for help. The connections we choose to make and tend in life are the web of support that can nourish and carry us through the darkest and most demanding events in life as well as the transitions from life through death.

My friend, Peter, who I owe the discovery of Oregon to, was an avid hiker, runner, and bicyclist his whole life. He was an ambitious man who made a name for himself and achieved success in his industry to provide the life he desired for himself and his family. His wife, Cathy, was his match and their lives were filled with love, community, and adventure. He was diagnosed with dementia in his 70's, a few years after overcoming prostate cancer. His progression over eight years was slow at first. In the last three years of his life he became very agitated about any change in his environment, acting out of anxiety or irrational self-defense. The things that he and Cathy loved to do together became distant memories. He tried to cope and self-moderate and Cathy learned to balance her needs with his. She was a resolute, loving, and resilient caregiver. Her devotion to him was clear, to honor all that he had brought to her life and what they had created together. Dogs were a very big part of their life and one of the greatest soothers for Peter as his Dementia progressed.

I remember spending time alone with Cathy, the last two times she came to Oregon with Pete. He was still ok in well-known places, like their second home here, but not outside of it. Any place that was unfamiliar, or moments out of routine, instigated agitation. She and I met for dinner. Although she is a great communicator with an open personality, it took some pressing to know how she was doing with all of this. Her stoicism is just who she is, an example to aspire to when life challenges occur. It was clear she was the one who felt most responsible for Peter, out of love and duty, even if she didn't get much time to herself. This was acceptable to her. She was soaking up her last days with the man she loved, even if he was different now. The day after they returned home from the last visit in Oregon, Pete had a stroke. It is hard to say whether it was imminent or provoked by stress. Dementia patients are very easily stressed and have a significant reduction in reserves for various forms of stimulation. He lived for a few more years, preferring isolation and comfort more and more. It seemed changes in his home were not as disturbing as being outside of it. His recognition of surroundings was still very personal and when construction began on parts of the home to improve access for both he and Cathy's needs, he delighted at the opportunity to be the boss once again, even if his directives were unclear. Pete was a joker and a strong-headed achiever. So many parts of him were still present, although confused at times. Cathy continued to savor every day and hold the dream of growing old together. As Spirit would have it, Peter succumbed to a rapid infection that prompted his sudden transition much sooner than Cathy or his family was ready to see him go. He passed at 11:22pm on November 22, 2019.

The outcome of Peter's transformation was inevitable and could not be prevented. They both knew what to prepare for at his initial diagnosis, but Pete was less and less aware of himself towards the end. One might see that the loss and awareness as the body and brain shut down is the sweet end, gifted to those who must endure the intensified progression of mental and physical degeneration. Being the witness of your own slow decay with age is hard enough to accept with grace for the cycle of time we call life until death. The release of a spirit trapped in the maze of a mind with decreasing room to move about, bestows the long-awaited freedom to re-integrate oneself with the creative flow of Source. It is a well-deserved transformation and healing for that individual and all those who have been witness or caregivers on this shared journey of devotion, compassion, and patience.

~ Nineteen ~

THE INVOCATION OF KALI

There are times in life where the darkest part of one's personal shadow must be faced and healed or released. Suicidal ideation may be the compulsion that fragments the image of an individual's sense of worthiness to live. Death as a mistress has its' own seduction, when perceived as a path out of life suffering or to another realm that beckons us back into the oneness of our origins before we were incarnate. The conceptual beliefs about morals, life, and death greatly affect how one feels about committing suicide, themselves, or losing a loved one to suicide. The deepest barrier in the psyche around most suicides revolves around forgiveness and absolution of shame.

If you have or are in thought about committing suicide- What can you not forgive yourself for? Where in your life are you struggling to cultivate tools and solutions to resolve and release shame or judgment? No one can answer this question but the one enduring the depression or reactive impulse to leave their body. Many therapies and spiritual teachings exist for the exploration of healing the wounds of our past in this life and those passed down through ancestral generations. If one has the will to choose their own death, then one has the will to choose their own life.

The harder truth in the multilayered factors of suicidal occurrence is that mental barriers to healthy choices for life are commonly attributed to major traumatic events with lasting imprints of emotional shock, addiction to substance use, or obsessions with ideas and relationships. Many suicides are ruled as accidents or the responsibility of the one who has transformed, by choice, is deferred due to substance use driving impulsive irrationality. What is forgotten or shamed in the reaction of others to suicide, is the choice made by the one who is lost to us that we feel is unacceptable. The ones left behind to clean up the mess and pick up the pieces, are engulfed by grief for their loss and the question of why death is better than life. This is intensified by their simultaneous grief as a witness for their loved one's despair. For many of us left behind in the land of the living, a loved one's suicide may find the least resolve of any other death we witness.

Throughout my life, starting at the age of fourteen, I have had a handful of friends choose death over life. The first was my sixteen year old friend, Frannie, who overdosed on opiates intentionally. I remember going down to see her after her first attempt 48 hours earlier. Her mom found her and placed her in a protective mental health facility. Frannie was so clear about her desire though. She said all the things the clinic practitioners needed to hear in order to discharge her. The day she was released she played out the same loving nonchalance and gratitude with her family. Then she went home, locked the door and succeeded in her second pursuit to leave her life for good. No one really understood why it was so important to her or what was so bad about her life. This is because we were not her and we did not see and feel what she did.

Another friend of mine, much closer than Frannie, had a hard, long fall-out in life. After a major bodily injury at work that led to opiate addiction for pain relief and financial instability due to disability, everyday life for him was a struggle to feel worthy. We were soul kin from the day we met and I am so proud of him in all the ways he pulled himself up from his bootstraps, got over his addiction, and went back to work after years of re-strengthening his body. Sadly, his return would cause another large fall with multiple fractured limbs because roofing and framing can be a dangerous job. When I visited him in the hospital, he was beside himself but talking optimistically. I saw right through it, hearing the shakiness of his voice and his darting eyes. He was in turmoil about repeating previous events of his life story.

I had already moved to Oregon and was only in contact with him by phone, off and on, after that day at the hospital. I saw him three months before he left this world, a year after his second fall. He was happy and seemingly his usual self. We went out for a long ride on his motorcycle around town, had beach time, coffee, and good food. I never sensed he was in a dark place, but when I got the call, I knew what had been ruled an accidental death wasn't. He hopped a bridge into a freight yard on his motorcycle, the last fall he would ever have in this life.

Intense emotional catharsis can leave us feeling empty and scattered. Multiply one experience that has been traumatic for you by 100 and a ray of empathy for the tortured souls who live in chronically abusive homes or war zones may shine a light on darker understandings. Veteran soldiers of any nation face a mass amount of death, violence, survivor trauma, and guilt during their length and cycles of deployment. Some never cultivate coping skills. Others were run ragged. Some may say there really are no coping skills that can resolve the cognitive dissonance of watching and taking part in that much violence and death when you have a mammalian brain.

It is a rare Veteran of War, who can take part in the ravages of the battlefield and come home to the simple roles of a domestic life to feel normalcy. The depth of blame, shame, regret, grief, and uncertainty of who they are and how to find a balance when accepting life and death can be an everyday cycle of searching. Those who have decided their role is to be in the war zone only, lead lives that look like this at home or seek deployment to calm their mind and trigger finger. Hypervigilance has become all they know. Although hard to accept, it is inevitable to see how this persistent processing of events and simultaneous attempts to re-integrate into the joys of life can be hard to grasp. No matter how much love, praise, and therapeutic tending is present to support them in finding other parts of their identity, they may never reach clarity in the maze of their minds.

I was a senior in high school when the War on Terror began. Multiple people I knew graduated and enlisted to fight. They all returned with deep suffering in part of their being. Randy and Tommy were the two to take their own life at the point of a gun. Both were under the influence of a substance, alcohol and painkillers, respectively. For Tommy, the pain in his body had become too much. The blinding cluster headaches after the sound bombs and other scars from flying shrapnel, deep in his flesh created searing pain. He was open about his shame, confusion, and guilt for the soldiers he couldn't save. For Randy, the shame and guilt ran deep and quiet. He was conflicted over whether to deploy again after two tours or to try and build a normal life at home. His death took place in the middle of an argument with his sister trying to talk him out of it. He had threatened suicide shortly before but didn't follow through. He said he wanted help but that had not amounted to much for him, yet.

Suicide is a salve for some, to resolve shame and pain, not to create more of it. It is up to us who are left behind to acknowledge the support we have given and honor the choices made by those who find death as a remedy for their unbridled pain and dissonance, rather than shaming their memory for it. Compassion for self and compassion for others, especially during loss, transformation, and death, may be the most beneficial teaching the Dalai Lamas have given us. This is the path to healing, acceptance, releasing what we cannot control or change, and honoring the choices we each face in the weaving of our own personal narrative.

Those who choose suicide are taking accountability for their own life by choosing death, as an early consequence. Whether or not you agree, it is not your responsibility to make them accountable for the life they left behind or their choice in death. You are responsible for the choices in your own life. That is all that is required. Reflecting in choices that others make creates a conversation with self, to witness and tend to your own decisions about how to live life and embrace death as a part of it. Respecting the choices others make in life is part of the learning process for understanding healthy detachment. This, balanced with loving offerings and negotiable requests, unveils the potency of exchange without dependency or expectation that others comply to your way, your beliefs, or your desires.

~Releasing the Bundle~

As we move through the experience of life and relationships, heightened periods of stress, conflict, and confusion build the perceived weight one feels in the heart, mind, body, and spirit. The myth of Atlas carrying the weight of the world on his shoulders is an archetype we all feel whether real or projected. The knots and tension of the spine, most commonly found in the mid-back and neck, are a signal for how one carries stress that affects the strength and alignment in one's being to "keep your head up" and move forward with a lighter step. The layering of emotions and thoughts that keep us toiling in our labor to achieve understanding, fulfillment, and resolve in the circumstances of life and death are a part of transformation within. Acknowledging when the bundle becomes too heavy is the most important time to put it down for a period of rest and relief.

During this timeout for self-care, objectivity and renewed inspiration grant the power to sort and assimilate the multi-dimensional factors requiring solutions. Sorting the bundle is necessary to assess what, how, and why one may be carrying responsibilities for others that are not theirs to bear. As empathic creatures we all feel one another, consciously or subconsciously. The closer the connection, the greater the call to be involved in other's perceptions, emotions, and conflicts in experiences they are having alone or relative to us. It is essential to release what we, ourselves, do not have power over, even when it is hard to witness. By doing this, clarity and accountability for how to honor others, create offerings without attachment to whether they are received, and hold integrity with how we are influenced to act or not act from our own thoughts and emotions, can be cultivated.

Directing our will to where it is most effective braids a continuous trust in the worthiness of self, empowers the recognition of what we are learning, and the release of what we no longer seek to carry. This is most applicable when the bundle feels too great a burden, depleting our reserves of compassion for self and for others and instigating cognitive dissonance. Engaging the alchemy of transcendence during times of anticipation for what is to come and times of hindsight in our review is the most potent approach to harmony and fulfillment.

~ Twenty ~

COVID19 PANDEMIC 2020: THE GLOBAL BARDO

This was the year I had planned to have this book written, the year I sought to unveil my art and poetry to the larger collective. The world's cognitive disarray, demands for change, and my own personal emotional experience required other investments of my time and focus. Being a witness and a guide in the immediacy of these concerns for my community and finding the stillness and inspiration within, were again required at another level of exchange I had yet to embark upon. Patience, compassion, and transparency was what the world was learning about, in order to overcome fear, doubt, divisiveness, and all the retaliatory thoughts and emotions that come when we feel a loss of control. All these things come in the phases of transformation that call for the acceptance of change with creative solutions to refine the forward trajectory of life as we have come to know it.

The same phases of experiential grief around death and life changes challenged the world all at once from the collective to every individual. The mounting pressure of processing life without normalcy and trying to regain a sense of what normalcy could be was antagonized by perceptions of death and loss, for oneself and of others. The concept of safety was torn in pieces for many and default coping mechanisms became the haven to survive the ordeal. The act of living turned swiftly, to surviving instead of thriving, with one National Broadcast to the communities it served. Simple arguments now magnified to war mentalities and "us versus them" attitudes began to infect many as they surfaced from the shadows of human consciousness. Some just froze and isolated in fear, others maintained denial of any concern at all, whether by acceptance of their own death and eventual species extinction, or by sticking their head in the sand because it was all too much to face. Many sought to inform themselves for clarity with basic acts of caution, while seeking a way that could bring stability and practicality back to the foundations of social and economic pillars in community.

The deluge of misinformation politically, scientifically, and socially only added to the unrest we all felt as it took center-stage as affirmative action, censorship, and control in ways that blindsided most of the average citizens used to being consumed by the drama or simplicity in the narratives of their own personal lives. The doubt and the clinging to the mast of authority for choosing what is best for the collective created more cognitive dissonance and compensation in the mind that solidified or completely turned over previously held beliefs. Doubling down became a normal response to conflict as the fatigue from processing all the thoughts and feelings coming through at once superseded compassion, curiosity with receptivity, and communication for situation specific resolutions.

It is possible that the enormity of this collective experience greatly influenced the intensified incentive to purge material

things, lifestyles, people, personal beliefs, and roles in community, more than anything else in the history of the last few
hundred years. One can only assess for themselves, the productive or non-productive changes in their own life outcomes when
reviewing current values and aspirations to refine the future.
This is the fabric of life we all take part in weaving. That is
why it is essential that we understand the difference between
human drives and soul yearnings for fulfillment and to learn the
alchemy of how these factors of being enable evolved consciousness. The goal is to not only endure massive life change individually and collectively, but to thrive through transcendence.
Transcendence maintains or restores a sense of wholeness. This
is achieved through cultivating the skills for experiencing life
changes and real or metaphorical deaths. Understanding transcendence strengthens foundations for more effective action to
create fulfillment beyond the perceived suffering of one's personal experience.

How have you healed from the perceived changes or wounds
brought on by the pandemic? How has this made you more of
your authentic self or taken you away from your authenticity?
How did you find a balance between honoring yourself and
honoring others in your world?

~The Hall of Mirrors and Self-Projection~

Awareness of self is an essential task and a skill to be cultivated for mastery of progressive fulfillment in our perceptions
of self, relationship with others, and accomplishments in the
world. Fine-tuning our awareness requires dedication and effort
to evolve with greater efficiency in our analysis of information

and the structures of belief we exist in and act from. When we turn our attention to the multidimensional concept of projection, it is like stepping into a maze of mirrors. Each reflection is a projection of self as it is, as it could be, and as one believes it should be. Then there are the reflections of possibility for how to receive and how to respond to each circumstance while the input of information from our experience is coming through. The program breaks down and defines the direction to lead our thoughts, emotions, and actions forward to manifest the next outcome in the narrative.

The hall of mirrors can be an overwhelming place, inciting fear and frustration that can be entrapping or too much to even enter, at all. Individuals that struggle with introspection, sorting, organizing, and coordinating the impulses that are innate to human thought and emotion will become trapped here. Resistance is a natural factor in the process of evolution. Resistance will arise as a subtle or intense pressure depending on the capacity of every individual to filter, sort, and organize their external life circumstances and internal perceptions of self within those circumstances. Whether or not one chooses to acknowledge projection as a gear in the mechanism of their life, resistance will exist.

Expanding one's clarity of how projections of self, others, and the circumstances one faces can reduce the experience of resistance. Activating this awareness protects and balances the amount of resistance from one's own projected perceptions that affect the outcomes and repeat storylines in their personal narrative. Projection can act to manifest outcomes in an individual's life that perpetuate or shift a narrative creating harmony or conflict. Once externalized, these projections affect our relationship to goals and connection with others. Understanding how projection is a major factor in every moment of our experience is essential to recognizing how our projections, clear or distorted, are serving or hurting us in our life.

Discerning projection is an essential part of overcoming guilt, resentment, and regret, and to find closure with loose ends. Discerning projections of self and others supports the path to cultivating peace, fulfillment, and gratitude. Engaging in this level of self-witnessing and accountability serves the authentic self within that seeks freedom and lightness of being throughout life, before death takes our last opportunity to inscribe this experience in the legacy of our embodiment. The Bardo is a Tibetan Buddhist concept comparable to other religions portrayal of the underworld or hell. The Bardo represents the known and unknown karmic field we are attached to in the life we have lived. It is a maze of pathways the soul must pass through in order to release attachment and resistance, in order to reveal the illumination of a higher path into the light of the void in creation. The smoke and mirrors of our experience in the secrets and conscious stories of the psyche can be misleading, delaying the transformation and transcendence of the souls return to the origin of all things. This is where the concept of lost souls, ghosts, and demons as a part of the underworld or trapped in between worlds, due to lack of fulfillment, is described.

If one denies the opportunity to sort out the resistance within and acts without awareness of self, any face from the maze of mirrors will opportunistically project. Most often, imprinted paths of response based on previous experiences will dominate one's projections in circumstance. These templates become malleable through introspection and awareness that allow one to define new structures of response. Then one may be compelled to act differently in the evolution of self-identity and empowered accountability for the narrative of one's life. As one cultivates greater awareness of self-identity, expectations of self and others, and programmed responses that influence perceptions and actions at each stage of one's journey, the potency of intention and empowered humility has the opportunity to build a healthy skill in the manifestation of experiences. This understanding supports the psyche's process of releasing karmic debt prior to the walk of the soul through death, enabling peace, resolve, and appreciation to lighten one's steps during the experience of living.

Projection in everyone's lives directly affects the collective experience we are all sharing. Resolving projection can be healing for every individual in a different way because of the reflections they see in their own hall of mirrors. If we each tend to accountability and integrity with self-awareness and healthy communication, we can transform the karmic field, known and unknown, in the collective experience of the world and society. Tending to projections allows us to heal and transform into a higher quality of being beyond these many metaphorical and real deaths we have witnessed together.

~ Twenty-One ~

THE WOMB OF THE PHOENIX

In late June of 2021, I began to feel knobby bulges in my pelvis, seemingly out of nowhere. I hoped for the best and prepared for the worst as I sought clarity in diagnosis. In October 2021, I was told I had uterine fibroids. With minimal diagnostics, the OBGYN told me they were benign but very large for my age and size, and a concern due to their rapid pace of growth. She told me to prepare for surgery in the next two weeks, to either remove the tumors or have a partial hysterectomy. My immediate response was to pushback and delay in order to research this diagnosis as much as possible. After all, I had only met this doctor once. It became clear that modern western medicine had little to offer besides surgery or hormone therapy, the latter of which I was told would not work for me.

As a practitioner of natural medicine, I am not opposed to surgery or the value of western medicine interventions. However, I do feel it is essential to apply my own medicine and corresponding dietary advice with reliance on surgery as a last resort. The call to surgery was too fast for me to allow with the assumption that there was no systemic threat to life. What we were discussing was the life or death of my uterus, a sacred part of being a woman, and at 37 years of age, a part that was still highly valued to me. "You no spring chicken anymore," my father's Chinese Medicine mentor, Dr. Chin, said to me, comically, the last time I saw him. I smiled painfully at the memory as I tried to talk myself through accepting that things like this are just a part of how we age, and we all face bigger challenges with our bodily functions as life wanes. This was clearly my burden to bear. It was a paramount moment to sort through personal biases, fears, and attachments about my body and sense of femininity, while safeguarding my authentic self.

With the first doctor, there was no empathy or discussion about the after-effects of this surgery or the risk that I may end up having multiple surgeries before menopause to remove the continual growth of other tumors. I felt like one of the many patients under my care, frustrated by the lack of constructive and educational communication in the American hospital system. It was now my turn to apply what I had been teaching them; how to advocate for themselves, get 2nd and 3rd opinions, and feel the answer in their body not just their mind, when it comes to decisions made for healthcare.

I was surprised when my emotional shock came at the diagnosis and recommendation. Planning and observing my body and expecting the tumor diagnosis the few months prior to getting in for an appointment, did not prepare me. As I researched more about cancerous and non-cancerous uterine tumors, it became clear that without a biopsy or glaring lab diagnosis proving extensive progression, there was no clear evidence from one ultrasound and minimal lab work that these tumors were without a doubt benign. The echo of my pathology professor's words come back to me, "Unchecked abnormal growth is cancer, whether benign or malignant." The medical field prefers to call malignancy "cancer" to ease the concerns of all involved, but any tumor can be a yellow or red flag for disease that eventually obstructs or compromises organs and tissues in the body. Had the Great Horned Owl in my sanctuary been trying to tell me something the past two years? Maybe this was my summons. I had to find a way to transcend.

I couldn't let that go. I had to be honest with myself, given the recent death of two aunts with cancer in the last three years. I could not pretend this was no big deal, like many I spoke about it with who didn't understand. "It's just fibroids." They would say. It was hardly real for anyone but me, including the health-care practitioners I saw that didn't believe I could palpate them, until they did. Then they realized how large the tumors were for my petite body and their empathy shifted in behind the mask of sterility. Emotionally, I tried to prepare myself for surgery while also intensively treating to reduce the size and growth of the tumors with strict diet and a large collection of herbs and supplements. The emotional tide came in waves, a tide pulling me under and bringing me back to the crest of a wave in surrender. How could I be sure I was making the right decision with the simple tumor removal and the risk of future surgeries or one surgery that would feel like a violation and unacceptable loss, requiring the forfeit of a part of myself that I loved and appreciated?

I felt alone in my process, even with friends and family to support me in different ways, this situation was about me and only me. It brought up all my perceptions and teachings of how to apply the skills for transformation and transcendence around change, loss, and death. My grief for my body was total. No matter what I did the tumors continued to grow larger. Over the course of five months they had begun to visibly protrude out of my abdomen. I was not angry or resentful of this happening. I was deeply saddened and disappointed that this could be happening to me after a lifetime of healthy physical choices to reduce inflammation and keep my body, mind, and heart in harmony. This was a part of my narrative and I had to accept that. Even more, I had to accept having surgery during a pandemic and the time to heal without a guarantee that my core strength and physical function would be fully restored. As an independent, self-employed woman, without a partner or a roommate to help pay the bills, I was being told to take time off life and self-procurement for a period of 3-8 weeks, depending on which surgery I chose.

Moving through the cognitive dissonance that comes when weighing these choices and attempting to acquiesce to the sharp edge of a knife, while being drugged into the unconscious, required many deaths, compromises, and refinements in my personal agreements with self. Honoring my emotions, holding ceremonial releases, and continuing to do more research for calculated decision making was essential to rule out regrets and heal resistance to transcending this experience. Preparing for the real possibility that I could die or have long-term sequelae from the anesthetic and/or the surgery due to my family history, was also necessary to maintain a sense of clarity and the will to wholeness in the conclusions of my heart and mind. I revised and prepared my Will & Testament accordingly, in order to ensure a legacy was left for those I love, and edited a Healthcare Directive to reflect my current wishes to protect me from unnecessary suffering if something went wrong. The logistical process of jumping through the hoops with insurance and medical care took more time than is usually expected. The pandemic regulations, backlogged surgeries, and personal crises or health concerns of the medical staff, plus the juggling of other general life events, provided an opportunity to practice greater patience, acceptance, and letting go of a need to control the unknown outcome of my story.

As the day grew closer to surgery, I had begun to look pregnant. The tumors were multiplying and enlarging to the point of compressing other organs. My head and my heart were clear, though. Through this ten month alchemical gestation I became very light and allowing of whatever would come from the next stage of my journey. Whether I lived or died, I knew this surgery would change me for the rest of my embodiment and reset conscious and unconscious codes in my spiritual DNA. The last decade of my life had brought challenge after challenge in acceptance, transformation, and transcendence in myself, my relationships, my career, and my purpose to the world. It felt like the gateway that was about to open, faced the abyss and I could not see beyond that vast empty space.

To honor myself, I had to trust that no matter what I had gratitude with no regrets for life, humility to be in service during this time of human evolution, and the wisdom of lightheartedness in times of hardship. I acknowledged and embraced these truths that had brought me so far in the ways of fulfillment and I stepped up to the threshold with intention for transmutation.

~Lightheartedness in Times of Hardship~

"*Ser Feliz Es Una Decision*" is the graffiti tag on a concrete wall in a lower socioeconomic neighborhood in Cancun, Mexico. "*To be happy is a decision.*" This phrase ripples with deep wisdom in times of hardship. It intersects with Buddhist philosophies about "*Life as all forms of suffering.*" and Vedic Scriptures that say, "*The pain is inevitable the suffering is optional.*" Statements like these may seem empty and myopic to an individual overwhelmed with emotional, mental, and/or physical hardship, but are they really naïve philosophies? Is all of life suffering when laughter, excitement, creativity, and success are existing possibilities? Is pain truly inevitable or is it one's perception of pain that is inevitable? The choice to be happy in the face of loss, failure, and decisive conflict throughout life requires the will to differentiate circumstances from a personal and impersonal viewpoint. This helps one gain perspective from emotional subjectivity and mental objectivity in order to strategize the steps for resolve, healing, and success. To move beyond the turmoil of hardships, the practice of acknowledgment and gratitude for the teachings of change and co-creativity must be balanced with the experience of oppression and demotivation. Herein, exists a doorway to uplift the heart and mind, to release the energy of consumption, and direct one's attitude and intention for creative solutions that are founded in worthiness and appreciation.

Lightheartedness is an invocable experience of feeling and thought. The science of meditation and attention to positive moments, affirmations, and actions such as smiling and laughing, even when the day or life feels heavy, activates brain chemicals that augment emotional states. How does it feel when you are lost in thought, walking down the street, and look up to smile at someone passing by who returns this smile of acknowledgment? How does it feel to push laughter out of your body when you are alone? Does it feel silly or empowering? If it feels silly you are still experiencing a lighter state of witnessing self than being caught up in the weight of cycling thoughts and emotions. It is important to engage that silly inner child during hardship. The inner child is where the vitality and passion we seek is found, in order to break past demotivating and judgmental blocks that come with processing life conflicts. This wholesome connection supports a way back into a flexible mindset. Being flexible is how one bends with the winds of fate or the consequences accepted by choices made of an individual's own free will. This opens the perceptive possibilities for creative solutions that expand one's vision for direction, to move beyond a predicament and enable graceful acceptance for the trade-offs that come in every choice one makes, as they navigate their own personal narrative.

Other considerations to shift mood include cathartic music in alignment with emotions for honor and release followed by reflective or uplifting music that inspires positive emotional states. Spending time with people, animals, or in nature that create opportunities to share the comfort of stillness or to feel loved and appreciated, can help redirect entrenched judgments about one's experience. Offering oneself these opportunities may benefit a sense of reprieve that brings objectivity. Reading or watching comedy can also be very soothing to a depressed and depleted individual if they are still above the threshold of apathy. When an individual is navigating their personal narrative with apathy the opportunity to move through life with curiosity, gratitude, and an openhearted mind are deferred. Apathy is the antithesis to passion and receptivity when an individual is depleted to the point of uncaring or choosing apathy to resist affectation. The point is not distraction. It is about intentional receptivity to the many shades of life and welcoming in the differentiation of an individual's personal and impersonal perceptions that can be cultivated as a reflex in the practice of uplifting.

Life is a practice. All the way through we meet challenges again and again that can frame behaviors detrimental to clarity, balance, lightheartedness, and successful creativity for self-fulfillment. Acknowledging it's a practice gives an individual the opportunity to choose what the goal of the practice is and how to live by this. Do you prefer to live in the practice of fatalism and victimhood and the practice of enduring suffering no matter the depletion of your sense of self? Or do you prefer to live in the practice of free will and discernment, and the practice of transmutation for gratitude and empowerment? The choice is up to you. Practicing lightheartedness in times of hardship may feel daunting or irresponsible to some. The lens of subjectivity, taking all of life personally and the lens of objectivity, removing self from any experience of affectation, are the extremes to subdue. Life is not personal or impersonal, alone. One's experience of circumstances will always present both personal and impersonal influences for perception.

How an individual is aligned, inherently and philosophically, on this spectrum dictates the perceptions brought into emotional and reflective awareness. Impersonal factors are discerned by understanding intentionality or un-intentionality from external factors or persons beyond an individual's control. It is key to understand what thoughts or emotions are superimposed but not originating from self and the framework of circumstances causing compensatory conflict for anyone subject to those circumstances. By witnessing one's orientation, historically and in the current context of experience, an individual may consider the practice of weighing personal and impersonal perceptions, in order to balance the act of honoring evoked emotions while transmuting impersonal factors that block the path to fulfillment and resolve.

In any given circumstance when conflict arises, there are wants and there are needs. The array of misperceptions, projections, assumptions, and ideals are there to be reckoned with. All of these components must be processed and sorted to evaluate factual evidence and differentiate philosophical truths. Depending on an individual's alignment, the pain and suffering felt from a lack of fulfilled needs and wants will perpetuate when clarity is mired by misperceptions that are caused by unacknowledged blocks and clinging to what is unfulfilled. Working with absolute needs is essential to defining the boundaries of the conflict and how to proceed with creative solutions in order to seek the achievement of those needs. Defining wants feels more negotiable to a circumstance than essential needs. Every individual must assess with willful honesty in self what defines a true need versus a want.

Whether an individual is aligned to the philosophy of resistance and loss or the philosophy of learning receptivity and gains, will determine the default mindset and behaviors they engage an experience from. Fairness is a philosophical ideal in human conceptualization that reaches for balance, but balance is a dance of trade-offs in the navigation of one's personal narrative. Fairness is dependent on shared perceptions of balance and the defined rules of engagement in society or in every relationship that is agreed upon. Without agreements for definition on equalization or mutuality, fairness cannot be met. This leaves the dance of trade-offs and the acts of free will as the primary framework for finding lightheartedness in times of hardship. Resilience is marked by healthy passion and will power that require a flexible mindset for adaptation in factors beyond one's control. It requires receptivity to creative solutions, perceptible in the field of knowing, that empower acts of transmutation and self-fulfillment. When given attention, the authentic self will radiate light and clarity to disperse the storms of confusion, resistance, and despair. The practice of life is what forms the foundation and constitution of the self, again and again. Rebirthing one's constitution beyond foundational childhood influences and experiential outcomes from any phase of living is made possible for every being that acknowledges a choice in how they perceive, manage, and accept the trade-offs in times of hardship.

How do you want to live life? How do you want to perceive yourself when you reflect on your choices in life and the foundation of that constitution that defines you in the world? The origin of this truth comes from within. It is nestled in the softness of the childlike heart, enveloped by the weathered hands of a wise elder. The inner spark of creativity in every individual is the same. How it is nourished, formed, illuminated, and radiated is up to you.

"Choose laughter with tears of appreciation, smile upon your own self-worth, and claim your story with curious reflection. Embrace graceful knowing that you define the most essential trade-offs of your own heart and soul."

EPILOGUE:

Choosing Love as a Legacy

The paths we take in life are initiated by fate and free will. The emotional experiences one perceives affect one's sense of completion or lack of resolve. Finding fulfillment or reaching closure in each experience enhances a sense of contentment that inspires us to move forward with empowered curiosity through the changes each path presents. Experiences that result in a lack of resolve may spur one forward onto new journeys as well, yet the quality of this emotional void calling for fulfillment and closure requires many coping mechanisms to be learned or employed. As life unfolds considerations about one's personal narrative arises in alignment with events that define new stages of growth and accomplishment or disillusion and loss. The wake of satisfaction or unresolve one sees reflected in their path invokes thoughts and feelings about the legacy they are imprinting on the world and those they share it with. Choosing to share a legacy of love is the greatest gift one can give to others and to oneself.

The mantras we carry every day in our heart and mind dictate many aspects of what we create and how we perceive opportunities for resolve or fulfillment. Mantras in the mind are repetitive loops and phrases one tells themselves. These mantras may be provoked as a natural response to an experience or invoked as an affirmative choice within that experience. Mantras may create positive or negative reinforcement about one's perceptions of self, others, and life circumstance. Acknowledging the mental loops that occur when processing an experience allows one to question the deeper implications and evidence for where those thoughts come from or how they do and do not serve outcomes for self-resolve or fulfillment. We each have the power to master the feeling of authentic resonance with affirmations that are founded in compassionate strength to endure and create greater opportunities in learning how to problem-solve. This ability empowers many skills for life success. It is essential to choose the mantras we live by with attention to how they affect our personal narrative and the legacy one intends to create. The reinforcement of opportunities through problem solving engages the creative mind and inspires the heart's curiosity. Love inspires the creative fire within to discover more fulfilling solutions. Affirmations of compassion and strength to endure fortify access to one's will power and support the heart-mind relationship to stay intact and focused. These types of mantras help one design their own legacy of love, reminding one of their authentic self when the experience of burn out, disillusionment, or loss occur.

There are many ways to experience and share love. How we place conditions on love, structures the way we share it with ourselves and with others. Love creates a potent bond, fortifies memories to cherish, enables receptivity for healing, and fuels the integration of personal growth in an elevating way. How one tends to the love they create is reflected by the relationship with oneself, others, and what one seeks to cultivate in the world. Love flows until it is put into form or rejected from an experience. Circumstance sets the stage and conditions placed on love, by those involved, are the governors of what someone gives or receives from that experience. Compassionate forms of love can teach us how to embrace an experience and how to cultivate non-attachment to fixations of desire when separation or endings occur. When a legacy of love is chosen, one intends to resolve disharmony to maintain connection or seeks closure for release that resonates with compassion and gratitude for the shared experience. Someone with deep abiding love and gratitude in their heart embraces all experiences as opportunities to grow. They understand this is the way to tend to the essence of love for self, others, and the world.

The path to sharing love requires a willingness to be vulnerable with an open heart and trusting in the resilience that is bestowed by practicing lightheartedness in times of hardship. This path presents the opportunity for profound discernment about what happens to love for self, others, or any attachments we carry when the impulses for self-sacrifice or martyrdom arise. It is up to us to re-assess the investment we have in thoughts and feelings that loop in the mind, heart, and soul. Experiences of resolve and completion are more likely to be achieved as one navigates their personal narrative with intentional awareness. By refining beliefs, ideals, values, and behaviors we effect experiential outcomes. The mantras we live by and act from have the power to lead us into bondage or to set us free. Choose your mantras wisely. Choose love as a legacy.

"WHY BIRDS SING AT DAWN"

Silence beckons,
    in the darkness- a resonant undertow
        so strong, that even the tallest mountains shiver.
    The cave of their mouths- gulping for air
        bellowing groans of defiance and acquiescence-
            to the rhythms of beautiful tragedy.

Cold stone only shines in the sun.
    The undeniable shift of light-
        always comes- with the most quiet "Boom!"
            an intangible bass- only felt by the heart.
    Knights in color- roll out the carpet
for Dawn to arise- crawling out of the void
    at the end of her journey to the other side.
    A radiant rebirth for all to share-
        no matter the weather- dressing her form.
    Ascending the tumultuous tides with humility.
        Embracing brilliance in the shadows of doubt.

A flutter of wings-
reach the heights of forest canopy-
    aligning their keel with the light of day-
in praise- adoration- chattering soliloquies.

The age of their wishbones glowing- in appreciation.
The call of their voices- echo
        In the ears of the world.
A triumphant brigade- marking the magic-
        This one moment of pinnacle meaning-
                a keynote revealing- the will to persevere.
A symphony of gratitude- to salute-
        The eternal wisdom of change-
                and you ask me-
                        Why do birds sing at dawn?

                                    -Julie J Hightman

A METAPHOR FOR CHANGE:

"Butterflies"
A Papago Myth

"One day the Creator was sitting, watching some children play in a village. The children were laughing and singing. Yet, as Creator watched them the Creator's heart was sad. Creator was thinking: "These children will grow old, their skin will become wrinkled and their hair will turn gray. The young hunters will no longer be able to hunt and the girls will no longer dance. The playful puppies will become blind and still." Creator thought "Those awe inspiring flowers in all their colors of red, blue, purple, and yellow will fade. The trees, standing tall and strong, will fall and dry up. The Creator grew more and more sad. It was in the Fall and the anticipation of Winter cold made the Creator's heart heavy.

Yet, it was still warm and the sun was bright, casting shadows and sunlight on the ground in playful ways. Creator took in the blue of the sky and the whiteness of the cornmeal the women were grinding. Creator smiled, knowing what to do. "All the colors in the world should be preserved." The opportunity to make something new and bring joy to Creator's heart, the hearts of the children, and hearts of the elders was uplifting.

The Creator took out a bag and began to gather, a ray of sun, a handful of sky, the dust of the cornmeal, a shadow of the little ones playing, the lush black of a fertile woman's hair, the rust from the falling leaves, green from the tall pine, the many shades of purple and red from the flowers, and even the songs of the birds. All these went into Creator's sacred bag.

Creator walked toward the village calling to the people, raising the bag as an offering, telling them to open it, to discover the gift. Some children opened the bag, laughing with excitement as hundreds of butterflies fluttered out around them and around the people of the village, landing on the trees and the flowers, their color was so breathtaking. They had never seen anything so beautiful.

The butterflies started to sing the songs of the birds and the people were enchanted. The songbirds listened with curiosity. One of them flew to the Creator's shoulder, upset, saying, "It is not right that you have given our songs away. You told us every bird would have its own song and it would be only theirs. Why have you given our songs to these new creatures? Isn't it enough that they carry all the colors of the world and dance in the lightest of ways?

"You're right." said Creator. "There is one song for each bird and I should not have taken what belongs to you. The message of the butterflies will be seen and known without song." Creator looked upon the world in silence taking in the goodness of all things.

-This story has been shared from many sources.

ABOUT THE AUTHOR: THEN TO NOW

Julie Hightman began her journey as a Holistic Healthcare Professional in 2004. Her focus on volunteering and treating addiction, abused women, veterans returning from war, and hospice have brought her many stories and experiences as a witness and facilitator of healing. Her offerings as a writer and an artist are another essential outlet for the passion and creativity she seeks to share with the world.

Author of the Poetry Collection "Seasons of Witnessing" and "The Weighted Feather: Essays for Alchemical Living and Empowering Mindfulness", Julie's message to the world is always one of curiosity, cathartic surrender, self-refinement, and the practice of savoring gratitude.

If you want to know more about her offerings or stay connected to new reflections and empowering practices, stay tuned via

www.FaizHealing.net   www.FaizHealing.com

www.ingramcontent.com/pod-product-compliance
Lightning Source LLC
Chambersburg PA
CBHW030306130626
46549CB00002B/713